At HOME With GOD

A parents' guide to raising spiritual giants

OLLY GOLDENBERG

Printed in the United Kingdom by Bell and Bain Ltd, Glasgow

First Published, 2019
ISBN: 978-0-9928184-5-6

Children Can

   BM Children Can
   London, WC1N 3XX
   United Kingdom

www.childrencan.co.uk
info@childrencan.co.uk

DEDICATION

To my parents. For your example, your unconditional love, your unwavering faith and your immeasurable legacy to me, which I appreciate more every day. I love you.

CONTENTS

ACKNOWLEDGEMENTS

When writing a book there are so many people to thank! While this may not be the most interesting page in this book, it is the most important page for me, personally. Without the following people, not only would this book not exist, my life would be by far the poorer.

Firstly, my thanks and praise go to God. He has blessed me beyond what I could expect and continues to reveal layers of His glory in a way that gently draws me closer. Thank you for your faithfulness and for the blessing of family.

To the church communities we have been blessed to be a part of. Kensington Temple, St Pauls Ealing and now Sunnyhill Church in Poole. You are more than a community or a place of worship, you have become family to us. Thank you for your encouragement and for always cheering us on.

To Tim Pettingale, editor of nearly all our books and helper in so many ways. To Stefan, your covers are always outstanding. To Alistair, you have blessed and supported us in so many ways, I don't know where to start, so this will have to suffice: Thank you.

To my five children. You have allowed us to experiment with the principles in this book. You have made the journey a joy. You have enriched me. I am proud of who you are and who you are becoming. Keep pursuing the King.

To my wife's parents: Colin and Jean, you have passed on so much to Helen that has made her the woman I fell in love with. Thank you for your wisdom, love and support. Your model of marriage has helped make ours a delight.

And finally, thanks to my wife, Helen (not to be confused with my mother Helen, or my fictional daughter, Helen). My best friend on this journey. I am in awe that God put us together as friends and life partners. Thank you for releasing me, no matter the personal cost to you. Thank you for your strength in times of struggle and your faith in God. This book has really been co-written with you, because although I have put the words on paper, you have put the principles to work in the lives of our fantastic five. Thank you for being more than I could ask for.

INTRODUCTION

Grand ideals

We all start off with big dreams for our children... They will make a difference in this world. They will be model children, full of character and love. They will excel at everything they do and go on to lead healthy, successful lives. They will love God and enrich the lives of others.

Parents don't tend to look at their new born baby and say, "This person will be a waste of space and a trouble maker."

However, in the busyness of modern-day living, it is easy for this early aspiration to be pushed to one side and replaced by a new, lesser aspiration: *survival*. Our expectation that, "My child will be a spiritual champion" quickly changes to, "I just want to leave the house on time, with my child wearing clothes that kind of match, are on the right way, and look reasonably clean!"

At one camp I was asked to lead a seminar for parents. Their children were all in a wonderful programme, where I knew that the leaders longed for them to meet with God. I started off by asking the parents if they had been praying for their children during the camp. Quite a few hands went up.

"What have you been praying for them?" I asked.

Each person took turns to share.

"I'm praying that my daughter will settle."

"I'm praying that they will have a good time."

"I'm praying that they will make friends there."

"I'm praying that my son will behave."

Not one person said they were praying for their child to meet and grow with God! As parents, it's so easy for our primary concern to be our child's external behavior, rather than their internal desire for God. We are more inclined to ask Sunday School leaders, "Did my child behave?" or "Did they make friends?" than, "Did they engage with God?"

I totally get it. To be honest, even writing this now, I know I do the same thing. I know how easy it is for our ideal desire to be buried under the everyday thing we call *life*. Any time we stop to think about what we *should* be doing, guilt can overwhelm and paralyze us, preventing us from moving forward. Or, we find that our well-intentioned ideas for change fizzle out after three weeks (or even three days!) as life takes over once again.

Yet, as I have travelled around and stayed in many Christian homes with grown-up children, I have discovered two distinct groups of families – those whose children are following the Lord and those whose children are not.

Interestingly, the distinction between those who do and those who don't, does not correlate with their parents' fervor for God, the stability of their home life, or their active involvement in the church.

Reflecting on the differences in these families I realized that I want to go a step further with my children. I don't simply want them to "stay Christian" as they grow up. My vision for them is not that they will *survive* church into adulthood. I want them to live as spiritual champions in the world and raise another generation of spiritual champions after them! I don't want them to simply live life, but *experience* life in all its fullness.

Even if I don't know all the answers, I know that I feel the same way as Joshua:

> *"As for me and my house we **will** serve the Lord."*
>
> (Joshua 24:15)

Reinventing the wheel

To do this, we don't need to reinvent the wheel. You may have been blessed with a Christian upbringing and have rhythms from your childhood that you can bring into your parenting. Conversely, you may be the first generation of Christians in your family. Whatever your background, you don't need to grope around in the dark trying to work out how to bring your faith into the heart of your home. In this book we are going to look at some simple principles that God has laid out in Scripture for us to follow. The principles shared in this book have been tried and tested over thousands of years.

For centuries, Jewish families have been following these principles, recorded in the Old Testament. Throughout this book we will be looking at the practical things Jews do to implement God's commandments, and we will learn from their tried and tested methods. After all, the concept of family did not begin in the New Testament – it has always been a part of God's creation covenant.

These principles have been used by Jews to pass on their faith throughout the generations. Better still, they do not require another three nights each week, an extra two hours per day, or a degree in theology to execute – which I'm sure most exhausted parents will be relieved to hear! These are things any parent can do, even amidst the busy life of the modern family. All they require is a conscious decision to give these principles a go (and an occasional reminder to keep giving them a go). They are things you can do in your normal, everyday family life.

While considering these principles, remember that every family does things a little differently and that is OK. Each chapter ends with some thoughts for you to ponder, either on your own or as a whole family, as you work through how to implement these principles in your home.

Let's begin at the beginning.

At home with God

PART 1

THE RHYTHM OF FAMILY

1

INTRODUCING FAMILY

God believes in you

In the beginning God made Adam and Eve and told them to have children. The very first social unit God created was the family. It was His idea. God gave parents responsibility for their children. He expected them to raise their children to follow Him.

You may feel overwhelmed. You may doubt your ability to do this. But God believes in you! God thinks you are up to the job. He knows your children's personalities, He knows the challenges, and He knows their future. God decided that *you* were the best person to raise your children and help make them everything they are called to be.

Throughout Scripture we see a pattern of God choosing the parents of those people who were destined to impact nations. Many times we read how God tells the parents about the future destiny of their baby. Then fast-forward a couple of verses and the baby has grown up and is now fulfilling the calling that God spoke over them.

When God looked at Samson, He knew just the right parents for him – those who would allow his fiery temperament to be maintained, so that when Samson grew up he would cause problems for the Philistines. I wonder if the other parents in the "mother and toddler group" looked at Samson's mum and judged her for the way she was raising her child? Perhaps they thought, "She's spoiling him" or "She needs to discipline him more."

God saw that Abraham and Sarah would be able to raise an Isaac; and that Isaac and Rebekkah would raise Esau and Jacob in a way that would fulfil His kingdom purposes.

In short, God has always chosen the parents who will prepare children for their future destiny. In the same way, God has chosen you to have the children He has given you. You may not believe in your ability as a parent, but God certainly does!

Taking responsibility

Eli, the high priest, had two sons, Hophni and Phinehas. They worked in the temple, but they certainly did not live for God. 1 Samuel 2:12 says, "Now the sons of Eli were corrupt; they did not know the Lord." God did not blame the temple teachers for failing Eli's sons. God blamed Eli for not stepping in to stop them. 1 Samuel 3:13 says, "For I [God] have told him [Eli] that I will judge his house forever for the iniquity which he knows, because his sons made themselves vile, and he did not restrain them."

Samuel's children did not fare much better. Samuel served God faithfully, but his children were not fit to lead: "But his sons did not walk in his ways; they turned aside after dishonest gain, took bribes, and perverted justice." (1 Samuel 8:3)

The Bible also has many positive examples of parents who passed their faith on to their children. Most notably, Paul talks about Timothy in 2 Timothy 1:5: "I call to remembrance the genuine faith that is in you, which dwelt first in your grandmother Lois and your mother Eunice, and I am persuaded is in you also." Paul saw Timothy as his spiritual son (1 Corinthians 4:17), yet in spite of this unique relationship, Paul credits Timothy's *family* for passing faith down the line.

You see, the first principle in faith development is that it takes place *within the family*. As parents we are used to contracting out many aspects of our children's development. The school deals with their academic life, the sports coach handles their physical development, and the church (by which we often mean the children's ministry within the church) is equipped to manage their spiritual life. But the spiritual development of our children is not something we should contract out to the children's ministry. As parents we must take responsibility for it.

We know that family is God's idea. In fact, it's so important to His order on earth that He chooses to put lonely people into families. (Not into church programs, social groups or clubs, but families). "God sets the solitary in families…" (Psalm 68:6)

For many years my wife, Helen, and I ran a large children's ministry in London. It was a very busy season of our lives, often working eighty-hour weeks. The ministry was very strong and we could see the children growing in their knowledge, desire and experience of the Lord.

I used to love coming home on a Sunday with my children as they would tell me what they had discovered about God. I remember listening with tears in my eyes as my four-year-old shared how funny his teacher had been in church that week. She had retold a Bible story getting the children to join in with silly actions. My son had loved it. Not only had he enjoyed it, he got the message – he understood something new about God!

But that's not why I was teary-eyed. As I sat there listening I was thinking about how the teacher had used the teaching materials I myself had written in my office, weeks earlier. The hard work of writing on my own had been used by this lovely teacher and it had affected *my* son.

A small part of me marveled at how many other children may have been impacted in the same way. A larger part of me, the part that was causing tears to well up, was struck by the thought that I had had a hand in helping my son grow closer to God (albeit indirectly).

When we left the ministry to take on a more itinerant role in the Body of Christ, we quickly realized that with our schedule, if we did not give input to our children directly, no one else was going to do it for us. For years we had signed up to the *theory* that, as parents, we were primarily responsible for the spiritual input of our children. Now we had to put that theory into *practice*.

This is not to say that we weren't doing anything before this. We were having regular prayer times as a family and were bringing God into our home lives in many ways. Not to mention the fact that the church community had been a massive part of our lives in terms of our relationships and our time as a family. But now we had to take on the responsibility God had given us to *actively disciple* our children. Our home would be the center point for their faith development.

I know many readers will agree with this principle. You may be chomping at the bit thinking, "I know *what* we should be doing. I want to know *how* to do it!"

In the chapters that follow we will unpack some very practical 'hows.' Before we do, let's make sure we are utterly convinced that God's primary plan for the faith development of children is in the family, and as parents we are called to take direct responsibility for this aspect of their lives.

This is not to say that there is no role for the wider church. No Christian family should be raising children in isolation from the wider church community. Yet, even in that community God intended the generations to mix together and to learn from each other.

Mixing generations

We'd been chatting with the pastors of a small church about the need for generations to mix together.

"Can you come and teach on this in our church?" they asked.

A few days before we were due to speak the pastor called us up.

"We had planned for the children to go to their groups during the teaching, but the more we thought about it, we wondered if they should stay in for the whole service. What do you think? Could you do the teaching in a way that includes them?"

I laughed. I was going to be teaching about the importance of different generations mixing together and we were discussing whether all the generations should be mixing together to hear the teaching! We were all certain they should be a part of it.

We put the whole congregation in groups around sheets of paper and asked them to list all the passages from the Bible they could think of where different generations mixed together.

The groups were buzzing as people from all ages were sharing their ideas. (The toddlers helped by drawing their own free interpretation of various Bible stories). The exodus from Egypt. The reading of the law. The feeding of the 5,000 (which should really be called the feeding of the 20,000 as there were 5,000 men, not counting the women and children who were there). The raising of Jairus' daughter. The teachings of Jesus. The conversion of the jailer and his household. The lists were long and included passages from most books of the Bible!

We then asked the groups to write down every time the generations were separated out from each other. You could see that even the most prolific Bible scholars were struggling to think of examples. One group declared they could only find one. I raised an eyebrow, as I hadn't managed to think of any.

"Go on," I said.

"Jesus separated the children from the adults when He called them to come to Him."

In this case they had to be brought by an adult, so other generations were represented. However, it did bring an interesting image into our minds of the children staying for real church with Jesus, while everyone else had to look on from a distance.

Another group asked, "Do times of war count? The young men went to war, but the young women and all the other generations were at home together." This was the only clear example we could find, yet here they were separated for function, not for faith development.

We then did a third study. "List all the places in the Bible where children's ministry is mentioned." If you do this study yourself, you will find that ministry to children is only mentioned in the context of the family or an intergenerational setting. To put it bluntly, the faith development of children takes place predominantly in an intergenerational setting.

While this book is not intended to be a treatise on intergenerational church, if you agree that this is a scriptural principle then we must consider the most natural intergenerational unit in the whole world. The place where different generations continually (and usually fairly successfully) mix, grow and learn together.

It's called *the family*.

The family is the easiest starting point for working out our faith together in an intergenerational setting. One family I know determined that there would be more of God to discover in the home than at church. This was not because their church was weak, but because they had made a decision that God would be at the very center of their family. Their children are now grown up and established in ministry.

This is our desire for our home. It may be your desire too, but what if it has not worked out as you had hoped?

I've failed

Before we move on to the practical things we can do to raise spiritual champions, some may be feeling like they have failed before we've even begun. Maybe you feel you have over-delegated responsibility for your child's development to the local church? Maybe some of your children are growing up disinterested in God and disengaged from the church community?

I think most parents feel like a failure at some point in their parenting journey. We judge ourselves harshly and, as humans, we tend to focus on our negatives. But remember, God believes in you.

Whatever your past looks like, whatever mistakes you have made (or think you have made), I want to encourage you that it is never too late to bring change. While some of the ideas in this book may no longer apply in your situation, you can still choose to be intentional in pursuing God's best for your family. Even if your children have left home, we can pray them back to the Lord who answers our prayers and pursues our loved ones by His Holy Spirit.

Whatever stage of life and spiritual development your family is in, you can choose to draw a line in the sand. We cannot change the past, but we can trust God with our future. We can choose to be deliberate and intentional in the way we disciple our children.

THOUGHTS TO PONDER

1. You may not know what it looks like in practice yet, but do you accept the primary responsibility for the nurture of the faith in your children?

2. What are you already doing to pass on faith to your children?

3. In what ways are you modelling living a life for God to your children?

4. What might intergenerational church look like within your family?

I choose to take my God-given responsibility to nurture my children's faith in God.

I decide to endeavor to have more of God in my home.

I declare that as for me and my family, we will serve the Lord.

"One generation shall praise Your works to another and shall declare Your mighty acts."

(Psalm 145:4)

2

TAKE TIME

The most valuable resource

Time is the most important thing we can offer our children. Through the time we spend with them they see our values lived out (or at least, our attempts to live them out) in a host of different situations. In the modern world, time seems to be the one resource that is severely limited. Yet if we are intentional about how we use our time, we will have enough time to plough into our children in an effective way.

I know this may sound like a fantasy to some. When it comes to time management, the reality for many parents is that we would like time to go to the bathroom uninterrupted! Why is it that our children always need us the second we lock the door? I remember the victory we celebrated as parents the first time we were able to get through a whole meal without having to leap up to get a cloth, catch a cup, or change a nappy. Add in a couple of (over)full time jobs, financial pressures, children's afterschool clubs, church ministry commitments and extra celebrations and it's a wonder we make it through each week with every child fed.

Acknowledging all this, I reiterate that we *do* have enough time to pass our faith on to our children. All we have to do is work out how it can fit into the natural rhythm of life. The way we do that will look different for every family.

Finding the rhythm

Occasionally there is a song that gets everybody moving to the beat. The rhythm of the song is so strong that it is almost impossible to sit still. Whether it is the tapping of a foot or a full-on body jive, everybody responds to the rhythm being played.

God has made life to contain natural rhythms. It is this rhythm which enables us to leave the house each morning with clothes on and teeth brushed, regardless of what time we made it to bed. The rhythm keeps us on track. The rhythms of our lives beat like a drum and set the pace for the whole family. Every family has a different beat to move to, but there are key principles that define this rhythm for all families. Jewish families understand this. For them, the rhythm of life is not simply a focus on our daily activities, it is a response to our Creator who worked on creation for six days, then rested on the seventh.

As we think about our family's rhythm, we need to ensure that God is included in every beat. Each day, each week, each year, the rhythm of our family should enable our children to move in step with their Creator as they grow to know Him more.

A daily rhythm

The first rhythm to consider is the daily rhythm. In a Jewish home the children would watch their father put on his prayer shawl and tie phylacteries to his forehead and arm as he prepared for prayer. For Christian families, this daily rhythm can be as varied as the family itself. For some it includes Bible reading and a prayer time each evening. For others it means worshipping God together in the car on the way to school.

Others may encourage their children to pray each day, as part of their morning routine, for as many minutes as they are years old. (This is a great way to help children take responsibility for their own prayer lives at home). One family I know do not leave the house until they have at least said a short prayer together for the day ahead. Many families will focus on the bedtime routine.

One family was struggling with their bedtime routine. They longed for their daughter to engage with the prayers and the Bible reading they were doing, but they found she was just using it as an excuse to prolong the bedtime routine, rather than an opportunity to meet with God. As a family they would usually eat supper together each evening. By moving their family devotions to supper time instead of bedtime, their daughter started to engage more meaningfully. Now, if they forget or are too tired, their daughter insists that they stick to the rhythm of a family devotion at supper time.

This daily routine may take an hour, if your family has that luxury, but it can also be a couple of minutes while on the move. What is important is that you find the rhythm that works for you.

A weekly rhythm

The second rhythm is weekly. For the Jewish family, the focus is on the Sabbath meal. Each week, at sunset on Friday, the Jewish mother lights candles and the family sits around the table as the father leads them in an extended time of prayer and fellowship. This weekly event allows the time for the family to pause, share, laugh and pray together. During this time family values are shared and family identity is built.

Intentionally setting aside time to eat together will enrich your family. I would strongly encourage you to plan a weekly rhythm of eating a family celebration meal together. Indeed, in our time-starved world this is the only aspect of faith development that requires us to set aside specific time each week. For many families this can take place on the same night each week. For example, Friday night is family night. Don't make any plans to move this night without agreeing it together. In our house, we chose Sunday night, as this works best with our family rhythm.

One large church took this advice to heart and the leadership decided that Friday night would be family night. There would be no youth meetings, home groups, band practices or any other activity organized by the church. Instead they would encourage people to meet, eat and share together as a family.

God commanded us to keep the Sabbath as a holy day. Whilst this is interpreted in many different ways by Christians, there is something about the weekly rhythm of having a special meal together that draws families closer together.

For those families where the parents work shifts, of course this night will change each week and therefore needs to be planned in. For a few families it will be impossible to do this weekly as a whole family, if one member of the family has to be away for prolonged periods. (For example, armed forces families, or those who work shifts on oil rigs). If this is the case, then work with the rhythm of your family. You may have long times away from each other, but you will also have long times together. You can build two different rhythms around these seasons. If you find you are unable to have a meal each week, apart from a few exceptional occasions, this should be a red flag for your family. You will need to pause and think what changes can be made.

So, what can happen during this weekly meal?

Many of the things you can do will be unpacked in the next two chapters, where we'll discuss the power of blessing and talking about God. At this point I simply want to encourage you to make it a celebration. Prepare special food, bring out the special crockery, use serviettes, make it a three-course meal. Do something to mark this day as a special day of celebration.

For centuries, Jewish families all over the world have celebrated the Sabbath and passed on traditions through their family. In the same way that many Christian families have traditions for Christmas and Easter, some traditions of the Sabbath are unique to individual families, while others are more universal among the Jews.

What are the core parts of a Sabbath day celebration at home? The Jews begin their evening meal with prayer around the table, usually led by the mother. They light candles on the Sabbath day as a visual metaphor to welcoming the light of God into the home. This is a practice we have adopted and that our children enjoy. It has created a memory they will carry into adulthood.

The Jews use this meal as a start to their Sabbath day. This is a day of resting together. Resting with God and with each other. Some Jews can be legalistic about this. One family would not place the candles on the table, but instead put them on the side, because once the Sabbath began they were not allowed to do any work, and moving the candles would count as work. Others employ a gentile to turn on the lights for them, so that they are not the ones doing the work, so keen are they to keep God's commandment. These anecdotes can be amusing for people who have not been brought up in the Jewish faith, but the principle of a day together as a family, without work, is vital for a healthy family.

The Sabbath is not a burden intended to stress us out, it is a gift from God. As Jesus said in Mark 2:27, "The Sabbath was made for man, and not man for the Sabbath." God has made us to work for six days and rest on one.

The Sabbath is a gift for us to enjoy. For much of my life I have endeavored to take one day off each week to allow my body time to recover. However, after a while, Helen and I noticed that we were using this day for all the housework that needed doing, and the small jobs we'd not had time to do during the week. It was not really a day of rest. We decided to stop and we gave ourselves permission to not work at all for one day each week.

On that day the dishes would pile up in the sink, the washing machine would not whir, the shopping would not be done and, most importantly, we would not feel guilty about this. We even chose to not cook, but to prepare our meals for the next 24 hours in advance. From our evening meal through to the following evening we would not work. By making space to rest we found we had more energy to complete our tasks on the other days of the week. We also found we had time to enjoy being with our children. As soon as sunset came, we could attack all the jobs that needed to be done with renewed vigor.

Now, in a different season of life and work, we don't feel the same need to avoid the washing machine and we are blessed with a dishwasher that can wash at the press of a button. Yet we still value the principle of taking a day each week to rest and be together as a family.

If you are not already enjoying a Sabbath day, I encourage you to give it a try and see what difference it makes to you and your children.

Annual rhythm

Each year the Jews celebrate different festivals. They have seasons where they feast and where they fast, but mainly where they feast! They have times to be together as a family. These festival days that God prescribed allow families to have fun together, but also to hold the Kingdom of God at the very center of them.

A Jewish family may attend the synagogue at Passover time, but they will also share prayers and a meal at home to celebrate Passover. When we understand the principle of this rhythm, we can see how healthy it is to set aside times for extra celebrations with God.

These may be built around the Christian festivals of Christmas, Easter and Pentecost. They may include elements of celebration from the Jewish feasts. However, your family chooses to celebrate God in the home each year, let this annual rhythm excite your children.

We celebrate Passover together (which takes place around Easter time) as we think about how Jesus became our Passover lamb to take our place. One of my children read about Passover in the Bible and asked, "Dad, is that what we do at home, when we get to hunt the bread and win a chocolate egg?" The excitement on his face was obvious.

Many Christian homes will celebrate Christmas together. The family rituals and routines all become an important part of childhood and family identity. Build times into your year where you celebrate God in the home in a way that is fun, meaningful and memorable.

This annual rhythm includes holiday times. Whilst financial constraints can make it hard to travel far for a holiday, even a week's camping will be a great bonding experience as a family. When on holiday our children get to see us relaxed and unstressed by work. We get to enjoy activities with them and spend time with them in a way that is not possible during a normal week.

These times also allow us to take stock of the past year. Many people use the new year as a time to reflect on how the past year went and to look ahead to the future; to see where our children are thriving and where they need more encouragement to shape their character for the future.

Annual rhythms act as bookmarks in the year. They are highlights that can be anticipated and reminisced. I will speak more about these annual rhythms in Chapter 6.

Other rhythms

The nation of Israel was also commanded to have a 7-year rhythm and a 50-year rhythm. Every seventh year would be a 'Sabbath year,' where no regular work would be done. During this Sabbath year, special devotion would be given to the Word of God, with the Law being read out to all people, including the youngest of children (Deuteronomy 31:9–13). This principle has led to some taking sabbaticals as an opportunity to rest, reflect on, and reassess life.

After seven sets of seven years there would be a "double Sabbath year" (Leviticus 25:8–12). This year was known as the year of Jubilee. It was a once in a life time experience – a special year when restoration would take place for the people of Israel. Israelites who had sold themselves into slavery would have to be freed. Fields that had been leased would have to be returned to their original owners. It was like pressing a huge reset button.

This resetting of life is something Jesus wants to do for every single person. His first sermon recorded in Luke 4:18–19 quotes from Isaiah 61, which speaks of this year of release. Hence, Jesus is described as our Jubilee. The day when we discover Jesus as our Savior is a landmark year for the rest of our lives.

One of the alternative rhythms we have in our family is to go out with each of our children on their own. With five children, having time with mum or dad on their own is a real treat for them and us. It takes us around 6 months to work through all our children and every time it is a rich experience. For us, this is an important rhythm, because we don't just want to help our children, we want to connect with them and understand their hearts.

The prophet Malachi refers to this act of parents turning their hearts towards their children, and vice versa, in Malachi 4:6: "And he will turn the hearts of fathers to their children and the hearts of children to their fathers, lest I come and strike the land with a decree of utter destruction." When we hear what is on our children's hearts and make a connection at that level, we are better positioned to help them grow into their destiny. As with other aspects of faith development and parenting, we aim to be very intentional about this and build it into our rhythm of life.

THOUGHTS TO PONDER

Think about how God is involved in the rhythm you have as a family at the moment. What would you like to change?

1. What does your daily rhythm look like and what would you like to do differently?
2. What does your weekly rhythm look like and what would you like to do differently?
3. Do you have a family day built into each week?
4. What does your annual rhythm look like and what would you like to do differently?
5. Are you due a seasonal change as a family?

Lord God, my time is in your hands. You know the seasons that you have for me and the way that you want me to use each minute of each day. I invite you to be in the center of my home and a part of all our activities.

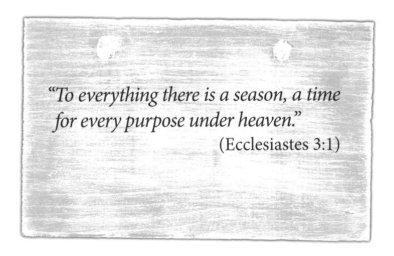

"To everything there is a season, a time for every purpose under heaven."
(Ecclesiastes 3:1)

3

THE POWER OF BLESSING

The revelation that changed everything

One day I had a revelation: When Jesus blessed the children, they were blessed!

Okay, I know that sounds obvious, but bear with me a moment while I explain. If Jesus walked into a room, blessed two of the people there, then walked out again, we would expect those two people's lives to take a turn for the better from that moment on, wouldn't we?

In other words, when Jesus blessed people, it was not a case of wishing the best for them, or even speaking a few nice words to make them feel well. Nor was it a superstitious act or a magic spell. Instead, it was a divine declaration that had the power to change the direction of a life. In short, there was power in the blessing that Jesus spoke: when Jesus blessed the children, *they were blessed!*

This is the Jewish understanding of blessing: it invites God's presence to come to that person or into a situation. As we pray blessings over our children, we are inviting God to fulfil His will for their lives.

Blessed in spite of the week

When we started to understand the power of our words in blessing our children, we decided to not only bless them on a casual basis, but to build a culture of blessing into our family. Week after week we prayed prayers of blessing over each of our children as we sat around the table for our weekly family meal. One week in particular we saw how significant this rhythm of blessing was.

It had been a difficult week. One of our children had been going through a phase recently and this past week it seemed to have gone to a new level. Every conversation with them was strained. Every request had turned into a battle and every conversation had turned into an argument.

Don't get me wrong, we love all of our children, it's just that we were finding it hard to get along with one of them at that particular time. Nevertheless, we chose to bless them – no matter what. Taking a deep breath, I placed my hand on our child's head, as is our custom, and blessed them.

It may be that you have a week where you feel like all you've done is shout at your children. Perhaps that week some gross disobedience has been uncovered at school. At these times, our words of blessing become even more important for our children. We are saying, in effect, "Even though I know you have been heading in the wrong direction, I still choose to bless you." To put it another way, "I bless you because there is a better direction for your life than the direction you've been taking this past week. May my words of blessing open up the path for you to go for God's best in your life."

This is not a soliloquy to repeat verbatim to our children. It demonstrates the power of praying a simple blessing over our children, week after week after week. When the time comes for them to leave home, they will know that we are blessing them each week, even in their absence. When they face challenges in life, they will remember that God has called them to be blessed.

Weekly blessings

Every week, as Jewish families sit around the table to eat the Sabbath meal, they speak words of blessing over each other. Using the words from Numbers 6:24–26 they pray, "The Lord bless you and keep you; The Lord make His face shine upon you and be gracious to you; the Lord lift up His countenance upon you and give you peace." The father, or in some families both parents, pray specific prayers of blessing over each member of the family. As well as praying for the children, a husband will pray the words of Proverbs 31 over his wife.

Blessing their sons

The father will place his hands on his sons' heads and pray, "The Lord bless you with the blessing of Ephraim and Manasseh." This simple blessing is packed full of meaning. Ephraim and Manasseh were Joseph's children. Joseph's father, Jacob had twelve sons. Each of these sons became a tribe in the nation of Israel, but in Genesis 48 we read that Jacob blessed Ephraim and Manasseh.

He started by saying that these two boys would be like his own sons. In other words, instead of blessing them to receive an inheritance as his grandchildren, he elevated them to receive an inheritance as his *children*. Ten of Jacob's sons became tribes, inheriting land in Israel. Levi did not inherit land in the same way as his family, but became the priestly tribe, set apart for God. With Levi taking on this role, Joseph's tribe split into two to make up the remaining two tribes. *Ephraim and Manasseh were promoted beyond what they deserved.*

When Jacob blessed them he also reversed their birth order. Although Manasseh was born first, Jacob put Ephraim first and it stuck. Jacob was reflecting how God had elevated his life to be above his older brother, Esau, so he was passing this blessing on to them: *May you be lifted above the position you started in, by God's divine favor.*

Not only does the origin of this Jewish blessing hold the profound significance of divine promotion, but each of the boy's names contains a blessing that any parent would desire for their children. Ephraim means "fruitful." Joseph named Ephraim this because he said God had caused him to be fruitful in the land of his affliction (Genesis 41:52). So, the blessing of Ephraim is asking God to make a person's life fruitful – that they will flourish in everything they set their hand to. In some streams of the Church, they pray a similar blessing, based on Deuteronomy 28:13: "May you be the head and not the tail, above and not beneath, the first and not the last."

This blessing of fruitfulness is one that endures in all circumstances. It is asking for fruitfulness even in a "land of affliction", meaning even if our children are in a place where fruit does not normally grow. Isaac experienced this kind of fruitfulness. He planted in a time of drought, when everyone around him was struggling to grow food, but he reaped a harvest of 100 times what he had sown (Genesis 26:1, 12–14). *This blessing says, no matter what situation your find yourself in, may you prosper and flourish.*

Not surprisingly, the blessing of Manasseh also holds great significance. Manasseh's name means "causing to forget". Joseph named Manasseh this in Genesis 41:51, after Pharaoh had taken him out of prison and made him the number two in all of Egypt. Joseph was saying that God had enabled him to forget all the rubbish things that had happened in his family, and in his past, and helped him to move beyond them.

We know our children will face problems in this world, but it is a real blessing to not get stuck on these problems. Though problems will come in life, they need not derail us from God's destiny for our lives. *Our future will not be held back by past situations and mistakes.*

So, the blessing of Ephraim and Manasseh is packed full of meaning and significance. Imagine these blessings being fulfilled in your life and in the lives of your children. It is no surprise that many Jewish families pray it over their sons every week.

Blessing their daughters

Having prayed for the sons in the home, the father, or in some traditions the mother, turns to his daughters and prays for them, "May the Lord make you be like, Sarah, Rebecca, Rachel, and Leah." These four ladies were the wives of the Patriarchs and the mothers of the twelve tribes of Israel. Each one carried the blessing of God and lived a rich and full life. They grew to be strong, generous, kind people.

The first matriarch had her name changed from Sarai to Sarah. The change in name reflected a change in nature. Sarai means quarrelsome, while Sarah means princess. This blessing is asking for our daughters to move from a position of original sin, quarrelling with the nature of God, to one of royalty as a daughter of the king. *May you know God and live as His child.*

Rebecca's name means 'firmly tied.' This blessing is asking for daughters to be anchored to truth, rather than anchored to emotions, flights of fancy, or people. We are praying that *their anchor will enable them to hold on to God and that in turn they will act as an anchor for their own household.*

Rachel's name means 'ewe,' a female sheep. Genesis 29:17 describes Rachel as a lady who was beautiful of form and appearance. A sheep is both taken care of and becomes a provider to those around it. *This blessing is asking for beauty (both inner beauty and outer beauty) and purpose.*

Leah is well known as the one who Jacob was tricked into marrying. She was Rachel's older sister and was not as desirable as Rachel. As such, it may seem strange to pray the blessing of Leah, the unloved, over a daughter. In fact, one understanding of the meaning of her name is 'weary.' That's not a blessing you would want for your daughter! However, an alternative meaning translates Leah's name as 'wild cow' and this is a more likely name Laban would have given his daughter – the first a cow, the second a sheep.

Naming your children after an animal sounds insulting to a modern, Western audience, but still, in a few parts of the world, animals are valued more highly than women because they are seen as a source of blessing, provision and stability. Thankfully, we have moved into an era where women, created in the image of God, are taking their rightful place as equals to men. But the meaning behind this blessing is one of fruitful, blessed, provision – and it doesn't just mean having fruit and being provided for, but also to enable others to be fruitful and to provide for others. This then becomes a prayer for an overflow of blessing. Indeed, of Jacobs thirteen children (twelve boys and one girl), seven of them came from Leah. Leah gave birth to half of the tribes of Israel! *She truly is a great mother in the history of Israel, even if she was misunderstood by many!*

Of course, you don't need to use these set words to bless your children. As parents our aim is to always encourage our children to desire God's best for their lives. These words of blessing are more than a simple encouragement to "be your best". They carry within them God's desire and act as God's decree over our children's lives. To put it another way, God's Word in our mouths is as powerful as God's Word in His mouth. These words of blessing have power to change the direction of our children's lives.

Seeing them as God sees them

When we ask God to bless our children, we are really asking for His divine will and purpose to be fulfilled in their lives. Jesus came that we may have life in all its fullness, and we are blessing our children to have *that life*. After all, there is no fuller life, and no greater blessing, than a life which is spent doing what God has called us to do.

A prayer of blessing is not a hopeful wish. Instead, it is expressing our agreement with God's desire to bless our children. As parents it is easy to get caught up with one aspect of our children's behavior, while missing the many awesome things God has invested into them.

This is particularly noticeable at the toddler phase of life, though it is true at every stage. When a toddler throws a tantrum, it can be exhausting to deal with, especially if you are in a public place with all eyes turned to you, and you are keenly aware of the inaudible tuts of judgement from others. It is easy for the whole focus of the day to end up being about that tantrum. After the emotion of the moment, the main topic of conversation between spouses can be that major meltdown in the supermarket and how it can be avoided in the future. Yet, it may be that prior to the tantrum, the child had had a great day on swings in the park, giggling and making friends.

We can choose to focus on the 5% of the day during which our child was having a tantrum (because that is the part that required the most emotional energy from us) or the 95% when their gorgeous individual personality was shining through. As we bless our children it helps us to refocus on the 95% and to believe God for the best for our children.

Blessed into their next season

As well as the regular blessings, we notice key moments of blessing in the Bible. For example, when Rebecca left home to marry Jacob in Genesis 24:60; or when Laban said goodbye to his family in Genesis 31:55.

Whenever our children are moving from one significant season of life to another, there will inevitably be a degree of uncertainty and insecurity in their life. As we stand with them and bless them into this new season, we are giving them a number of benefits.

The first is to show our children that we believe in them – that they have what it takes and are ready for this next season of life.

The second is to remind them that, no matter what happens, we are *for them*, supporting them along the way.

The third aspect links with the spiritual significance of blessing discussed at the start of this chapter. When we bless our children into their new season, we are doing more than just wishing them well, we are preparing a path for them to walk in God's best for their lives.

Starting seasons

So what seasons merit our blessing? All of them! Many of the minor changes in life will be covered in a weekly rhythm of blessing, but there are certain significant shifts that will require a different way of thinking and being. These moments in life are like forks in the road, where our children could easily slip onto the wrong path or be more established in following God. At these key times we should be willing to bless.

1. **During pregnancy.** For more details on this aspect of blessing, see our book: *Jesus, your baby and you.*

2. **At birth.** Many cultures around the world have some kind of blessing ceremony at birth. Christenings, child dedications and naming ceremonies each mark this moment in a child's life and set them on a prophetic course for their future. Part of this blessing includes the name that we choose for our children. After all, this is the label that will be used to identify them for much of their life. Jabez reacted strongly against his name (meaning 'pain'), longing for God to set his life on a different path to the name he had been given. Meanwhile, God changed people's names to match their newly revealed destiny. Abram became Abraham; Jacob became Israel.

3. **When starting school.** One church community in Scotland blesses all of the children at the start of their school lives. On the Sunday before the school year begins, they invite all the children who are about to start school full time to come to church wearing their school uniform. For many of the children, this is the first time of putting on their school uniform to leave the house. This is a significant day! How many of us still have that first day of school photograph as we

stand shyly, looking smart in an oversized uniform of which we've been told, "You'll grow into it!"

The children are called to the front and the church community affirms and blesses them as they start their school career. I love this on so many levels. It says to the young people, "We're for you and this community is your home." It encourages the older members of the congregation to pray for the children at this life-changing moment. Above all, it invites God to be at the very center of their school career. In the same way, starting secondary school or high school can be another significant time of blessing.

4. **On reaching adulthood.** In our home we have a special time of blessing when our children arrive at the ripe old age of 13. (You can find out more about this in Chapter 14.) As they enter adulthood they are moving from the place where we have been primarily responsible for them, to a place where they will have to take responsibility for themselves.

5. **When they leave home.** A person's responsibility increases exponentially when you leave home. You soon discover that food does not prepare itself, housework does not automatically happen (have you ever visited a student house?), toilet rolls do not replace themselves, money only goes so far, and you are responsible for it all! Without your parents watching, you are also free to do whatever you want. Once again, this is a fork in the road. At this moment we, as parents, can bless our children into this season. We have invested much of our time and prayers into helping our children become the godly characters God has called them to be, now it truly is over to them to run the race.

6. **When they get married.** A happy marriage provides such a strong foundation for life. A rocky marriage can make successes won elsewhere pale into insignificance. What a great time for us to publicly bless our children, asking God to bless their marriage. Traditional speeches by the father of the bride allow for such an opportunity to be done publicly, but giving our private blessing to our children will also have a significant impact on their lives.

7. **When they become parents.** This is probably the biggest life change one can ever make. Even when you are married, you can still choose to leave the house anytime without planning. With children, however, you have to plan to be spontaneous, even with your wife/husband: "Let's have a spontaneous night out together. I've checked, and the babysitter is free next Tuesday!"

8. **As your final words to them.** Though none of us know when we will leave earth for eternity, it may be that we will have one final opportunity to speak words of blessing over our children, to encourage them that they have "got this" and can do life without us. Much of Jesus' plan for discipleship was to equip and prepare His disciples for a time when He would no longer be with them in the same way. This is just as true for us as parents. Many of the patriarchs in the Bible prayed blessings over their children as they lay on their death bed (or in Jacob's case, several decades before he actually died).

Let's plan to ask God's blessing for our children in every season and every situation. Of course, just because we miss one of these opportunities to bless our children, does not mean that their whole lives will fall apart. But remember, blessings are powerful: when Jesus blessed the children, *they were blessed*. The same is true when we ask God to bless our children.

THOUGHTS TO PONDER

1. Can you think of a time in your life when someone prayed for God to bless you? What impact did it have on you?
2. Do you have a rhythm of blessing your children regularly?
3. When is the next big transition that you can prepare to bless your child into?

Thank you, Lord, for the blessing of my children.

Help me to be quick to bless and slow to become angry.

May my children become all you have called them to be and fulfil your purpose for them, here on earth.

"The Lord bless you and keep you; the Lord make His face shine upon you, and be gracious to you; the Lord lift up His countenance upon you, and give you peace."

(Numbers 6:24–26)

At home with God

PART 2
GOD AT THE CENTRE

4

TALK ABOUT GOD

Every day conversations

When it comes to talking about God in the home, there are two extremes of Christian parenting.

In the first extreme, parents hardly ever mention God. If you are not used to talking about God in your conversations, then any conversation where He is mentioned can feel awkward – perhaps through a desire to not come across as being 'super-holy', or put children off God by talking about Him all the time. One minister took this approach. He was concerned that his children would overdose on God, so avoided any mention of Him at home. The danger here is that his children will learn that God is only a part of their dad's job (or that God is to be confined to the church building), as opposed to a part of everyday life.

The second extreme does not allow any conversation to pass without a Bible verse, complete with reference, being quoted. To avoid becoming worldly this household will ban any topic of conversation that cannot be found in Scripture. From sport to people's favorite food, all conversations will be frowned upon unless they include some spiritual principle. However, we should not avoid speaking about God for fear of moving to this other extreme. It is unlikely that you will ever have a conversation like this:

> *"Dad, I think my team are going to win the Premiership this year."*
>
> *"But son, are you aware that this is meaningless if they do not know the Lord?! Beware of the sin of those who have everything, as it says in…"*

Or this:

> *"Mom, can I go and play outside?"*
>
> *"All play is meaningless. Rather, we should be seeking to worship God wherever we go. If you would like to*

> *go outside to appreciate God's creation, then that is permissible, but if you will not consecrate yourself with an attitude of worship as you enter into the realm of this world then you will have to stay home!"*

Clearly, these stereotypes are quite ridiculous, but the fear of one extreme can drive us towards the other. The two extremes display the tension that many of us feel when it comes to discussing God in the home. On one hand we want our children to experience life in a similar way to their classmates, and on the other hand we want no part of the world's way of speaking. This is the very tension that Jesus spoke about when He told us to be *in the world*, but not *of the world*.

Having established that the home should be the center of faith development, clearly no subject should be off limits. God must not be hidden from our family life, but should be a natural part of our conversations. How can we help this to happen? Should we have set times when we sit as a family to talk about the things of God, or should we have a quota of God conversations per day to make sure that He gets enough of a mention? How can we talk about God in a natural way that will help our children to discover more of Him for themselves, and allows them opportunities to share what God is doing in them?

Deuteronomy 6:7 says, "You shall teach them diligently to your children, and shall talk of them when you sit in your house, when you walk by the way, when you lie down, and when you rise up." This verse forms part of a prayer that Jews say twice a day, called the Shema. As they recite it, day after day, it reiterates that faith is grown in the home.

This one verse shows us some principles that can encourage us to talk about God in the right way.

1. We should teach our children and not simply expect them to absorb faith by osmosis.
2. We should talk about God all through the day.
3. We should talk about God in everyday life.
4. We can be deliberate and intentional about bringing God into everyday situations.

Talking about the things of God with those we love the most should be the most natural thing in the world. If you are not used to talking about God in your home, then it may seem strange when you first start a conversation, but don't be put off by that. Any new experience feels strange until it becomes normal, whether it is starting a new job, driving a new car or introducing a new topic of conversation to our family.

If you are not sure where to begin, why not start by taking time over Sunday lunch to talk about what you have all learnt that day. You may already ask your children what they learnt at Sunday School, but you can also tell them what impacted you from the adult sermon.

Thinking about your life, you may wonder how you can have time to fit God-conversations into the day. Yet this verse makes it clear that *no extra time is needed*. All that is needed is for us to be intentional about allowing God to be a part of our conversation.

I have a question

"Dad, how does this work?"

"Mom, what should I do with this?"

"Dad, why do we have to do this now?"

Questions are a key part of the learning experience. When Jewish families celebrate Passover, the youngest child has a chance to ask key questions about the feast. Why do we do things differently at Passover? What's special about tonight?

This process of asking questions and finding answers is a key part of developing opinions. We may not have all the answers to our children's questions, but the very process of questioning is important.

One of our children's natural inquisitiveness leads to them dismantling items around the house to find out how they work! Many times he has come running to us with great excitement: "Oh Dad, I've just worked out that this is powered by a magnet" or "Mum, I've discovered how this works, but now it's not working!" The process of asking, discovering and learning sometimes involves "dismantling" things so that we can understand them more deeply.

Jewish seminaries, for the training of rabbis, are not quiet places. The students are encouraged to debate with each other the meaning of various texts. This process of challenging each other's views, and even having to find support for views they don't agree with, helps them to form their opinions after they have looked at the evidence from many different angles.

Education goes through different phases, from knowledge being imparted by a teacher, to students going on a journey of self-discovery. From being focused on passing exams, to being focused on developing a love of learning. When our children are asking questions, they are showing us that they are engaged and have a desire to learn; to have their opinions shaped.

That's the theory, but in practice it seems our children have a habit of asking questions at the wrong times. Two of the favorite times for asking questions in our household are when we are rushing out the door or when they are supposed to be going to sleep. Yet, these questions are evidence of a desire to discover and to grow closer to God. When we take them seriously, we are taking our children's faith seriously.

It's great to discuss our children's questions on the spot, when they are asking, but this is not always practical. If it is past their bedtime, then feel free to pause the conversation and take it up again the next day. It'll give you a great reason to kickstart a conversation the next morning, when you get up. (It'll also give you a chance to think through the answer, phone a friend and pray through what is the question *behind* the question they asked!)

When we encourage our children to think and question, we are allowing them to grow. Our conversations with them can work to provoke thought and interest. This is the model Jesus used when He told His parables. His stories were intended to provoke thought, which they clearly did because His disciples would ask Him about them. The stories in the Bible provoke similar questions today and can provide an opportunity for teaching, in the same way that stories in the news, or events that occur at school, promote discussion.

Opportunistic teaching

As parents, we are in a very privileged position. We get to see and know our children in everyday life in a way that no one else ever will. We see them in their triumphs and in their challenges. The best time to teach our children is during everyday life.

When our children are struggling at school, this is a great opportunity for them to learn to trust God in the hard times. When our children are preparing for a test, we can give an eternal perspective. When our children see others suffering, we can teach them about God's heart for those in need and this can lead us to action.

One evening, one of my sons announced to me, "Dad, God doesn't answer prayer."

I have to admit, I was thrown by the statement. This is a boy who has prayed for sick people and seen them instantly healed. This is a boy who has witnessed miracles with his own eyes. How could he not believe that God answers prayer? It would have been easy to shoot this statement down and shut down the conversation. However, while I would have been speaking truth, my son would not necessarily have been receiving it. So, taking a deep breath, I engaged in the conversation.

"What makes you think that? You've seen God answer lots of prayers in the past."

"I know, but that was in the past. He doesn't answer prayer now."

"Well, what are you praying for that God has not answered yet?" I asked, trying to understand how he'd reached his conclusion.

"I've been praying for my friend to come to Jesus and he hasn't. I've also been praying to get to know God more, and I don't. Plus, I've been praying to find my lost toy and I haven't."

Now I understood his frustration. God gave me insight into what was going on. He'd been praying one of those dangerous prayers. You know the ones: "God give me more patience." But God doesn't give us more patience, instead He sends circumstances that develop patience. My son had asked God to get to know Him more.

"Perhaps God wants you to know that He is not a slot machine," I said, "where you put a prayer in and get an answer out. Perhaps He wants to teach you that He is a person who wants you to spend time with Him."

My son looked thoughtful for a moment and that was the end of the conversation. Within a few days he had the opportunity to share the Gospel with his friend, found his lost toy, and learnt something new about his relationship with God. All this gave me an opportunity to reinforce our previous discussion.

The time we are most open to learning is when we need to know what we are learning. You can teach me how to change a car tire and I might think I understand, but if my tire is flat and needs fixing *now*, you can be sure I will pay more attention.

Jesus used this method of *opportunistic teaching* with His disciples. When they couldn't cast out the evil spirit in Matthew 17:14–21, Jesus used the opportunity to teach them about casting out demons. When the disciples had seen the power of God at work through them, Jesus encouraged them to keep their focus on salvation more than the miracles (Luke 10:17–20).

One family I know use this approach of opportunistic teaching, but also make a point of following up on what they speak about at a later date. If their children are praying for a specific answer to prayer, they make a point of reminding them what they prayed for when God answers.

If your children ask you a theological question, you can look for an opportunity to see the outworking of that theology in the world around them: "Do you remember last week when we were talking about why God doesn't do anything to help the homeless? We spoke about how sin is in the world, but God wants to work through His church to shine His light in a dark place. Did you hear in the notices how we are running a night shelter for the homeless in the church? That's exactly the kind of thing we were speaking about."

When God is involved in our everyday conversations, our children learn to grow with God, instead of apart from Him. When they can ask us anything they want, without fear of being shut down, we have an opportunity to speak God's truth into their hearts, right when they need it.

THOUGHTS TO PONDER

1. Do you have a particular time of day when you can talk about the things of God with your children? For example, on the way to school, or at bedtime?

2. How do you make space for your children to think and ask questions about their faith?

3. Can you think of a time when you were able to provide opportunistic teaching, using the situation around you to discuss or demonstrate a lesson of faith?

Lord, help my life to be a sermon for my children. Help our conversations feed their spirits. Help my ears to hear their questions, so that you can speak truth into the deepest parts of my children's hearts. Help my family grow closer to you every day.

"You shall teach them to your children, speaking of them when you sit in your house, when you walk by the way, when you lie down, and when you rise up."
(Deuteronomy 11:19)

5

MEMORIAL OBJECTS

Mirror, mirror on the wall

The mirror on the wall in our house reminds us of one late night, early on in our married life. Helen and I had recently moved into our house and had been working to redecorate the living room. Earlier in the day we had tried to put up a large mirror over the chimney breast. Unfortunately, we could not drill the holes. We even borrowed a builder's power drill, but all we managed to do was chew up the drill bit. The builder helpfully advised us that we would never be able to drill a hole where we were trying to drill it. Not to be deterred, we carried on with our redecorating as we pondered the problem.

As midnight approached, we had finished painting the walls and ceiling. We had hung the pictures up and fitted the light fittings. Everything was hung in place, except the mirror. That's when we came up with the bright idea of sticking it to the wall with glue!

Quickly, we dabbed the back of the frame with super-strong glue. Both of us pressed the mirror against the wall and held it in place to stop it slipping. It was only then that I looked at the instructions more carefully: "Hold in place for 12 hours as the glue dries."

Exhausted from a day of labor, we both burst out laughing as we pictured a sleepless night spent holding up the mirror. Helen was concerned that the mirror would smash to the floor in the middle of the night. I wasn't concerned that it would fall, but that it would slip down at a strange angle, fixed in place for eternity.

Helen then built an incredible contraption made out of boxes, broom handles and other available paraphernalia to hold it in place, and when we tentatively came downstairs in the morning the mirror sat perfectly on the wall, never to be moved.

Now we cannot look at that mirror without remembering that night. That mirror serves as a memorial of that moment. Visual reminders are a key part of reinforcing memories. That's why God constantly encouraged the Israelites, and all believers, to keep memorials.

When Jacob had a dream of an open heaven he built a pillar, laid a stone and changed the name of a city to mark the occasion (Genesis 28:18–22).

When God fed the Israelites with manna in the desert, He told them to keep a bowl of the manna in the ark of the covenant (Exodus 16:30–34).

When Aaron's rod budded to show that God had chosen his line to be priests, it was kept in the ark of the covenant (Numbers 17:10; Hebrews 9:4).

The Israelites were instructed to tie the law of God to their arms and foreheads as a reminder of the law (Deuteronomy 11:18–20).

When Joshua led the Israelites through the river Jordan, which parted by the power of God, he then instructed them to build a memorial. The purpose of this memorial was to provoke questions from future generations to allow the retelling of what God had done that day (Joshua 3:1–7).

When the Israelites living to the east of the Jordan returned home, they built an altar, so that if there was ever any doubt as to whether they were a part of Israel they could point to the altar as evidence (Joshua 22:21–29).

The temple was full of memorials and symbols to point people to God – from the clothing the priests wore, carrying the twelve tribes of Israel as jewels before the Lord, to the sacrifices they made.

All these memorials were intended to remind people, in the busyness of normal life, of the incredible power of God at work. Specifically, they were intended to prompt the retelling of the stories of God at work in the life of Israel.

Jesus set a similar memorial in place when He instructed us to take communion. When we do this, we are remembering what Jesus has done for us and we have an opportunity to explain these things to our children.

Memorials in our nations

Much of the Western world has been built on Christian foundations. Past generations shaped our government, education, hospitals and orphanages. Believers sought to help and support those who were the most vulnerable in society and the Gospel was preached across the land.

In the United Kingdom this heritage is visible nearly everywhere you go. In Bristol you can stand behind the pulpit where John Wesley preached to thousands of miners as they made their way home. In many rural places, school houses, orphanages and church buildings are still visible, as testament to the impact they have had on the nation.

In Bourneville town you can see the work of the social reformer, George Cadbury. Creator of chocolates he became one of the first factory owners to be concerned for the wellbeing of his workers. He built houses for them with plenty of green space, encouraged sports, offered sick pay and created funds to help families when workers suffered from long term sickness or died early. He transformed life for his workers. Others gradually followed his lead and governments eventually legislated for the benefits he introduced.

One day, I was walking through London with my children when one of them stopped and said, "Look Daddy!" He was pointing to a blue plaque that had been fastened to iron railings next to the walkway. As I read it, I felt a chill go down my spine.

> *"The probable site, where, on May 24, 1738, John Wesley 'felt his heart strangely warmed'."*

I had the privilege of standing in the place where John Wesley, the founder of the Methodist movement that was used by the Holy Spirit to change our nation, first encountered God. As I stood there, over 250 years later, I had to pray, "Lord, you poured out your Spirit on one person in this spot hundreds of years ago. Please do it again."

That memorial led to a greater desire to see God move again in our nation. Part of the reason why we wrote the *God's Generals for Kids* series was to allow children to know the history of some of the things God has done in the past. Jesus is the same, yesterday, today and forever. Knowing the history of previous outpourings opens up the possibility in our minds of what God can do in our time.

Our spiritual history is a pointer to our roots. Since the time when the New Testament was completed, the Church of God has not been silent. Instead, it has been progressively advancing towards its destiny as the Bride of Christ. We stand on the shoulders of those who fought for the faith in their time and we are surrounded by a great host of witnesses who are cheering us on.

Memorials remind us of our part in this long history of life and give us an opportunity to share these incredible stories with our children.

Memorials in our homes

If memorials have a key place to remind us of God's work in society, can they also have an impact in our homes?

Most families have photographs around the home. These are memorials to times past and to family members. They say something about who you are to visitors and build your identity as a family. That quirky photo from when your children were young becomes a visible memory in their lives, one which is reinforced daily. In the same way, we can have items that capture the God-moments in our lives.

The Jewish people were encouraged to do exactly this as they tied verses from the Torah (the Law) around their arm and forehead. They also placed a Mezuzah on their doorway. The Mezuzah is a small box containing parts of the Law. When a Jew enters a house, he will touch the Mezuzah and even kiss his hand as a reminder of his love for the law and his decision to follow it. In an orthodox home Mezuzah's will be found at the entrance to every room, except for washrooms.

Imagine going to visit your Jewish friend. You walk through the front door (*kiss – I love the Law of God*) and go into the hallway where you take off your coat. You then go into the living room (*kiss – I love the Law of God*) to take a seat. Your host offers you a drink and pops into the kitchen to make it (*kiss – I love the*

Law of God). They come back in (*kiss – I love the Law of God*) to ask if you want milk and sugar in your tea. Returning to the kitchen (*kiss – I love the Law of God*) they boil the kettle. Then they return with a plate of biscuits (*kiss – I love the Law of God*). Then they go back into the kitchen (*kiss – I love the law of God*) and return once more with your tea (*kiss – I love the Law of God*). Finally, they sit to chat.

This continual observance would help to keep God in mind throughout the day as you moved from room to room, visiting your friend. This was precisely the intention in Deuteronomy and echoes Paul's instruction in 1 Thessalonians 5:17 to pray continually. These continual memory-prompts direct our thoughts to God.

Of course, it can just become an empty ritual of meaningless symbolism. Dead religion has a form of godliness, but denies the power behind it (2 Timothy 3:5). Yet there is something to be said for keeping memory prompts around the home which are visible to all. Much of this is to do with our heart. In the busyness of the day we are all prone to forgetting about God.

The memorials around our home may be as simple as a Bible verse hung on the wall or a church newssheet stuck to the fridge. These items help shape our family identity by keeping our faith visible and central in the home.

Objects are not the only visual reminders that your children will see. When they see you reading your Bible in the morning, or know that you have a time of prayer at a certain point in the day, these too act as memorials for them that God is at the center of your home.

While I like to have time in prayer on my own in the morning, I chose to make an exception when my children were babies and they could join in my prayer time if they were awake. I wanted them to experience God's presence with me. As young children they would sometimes wake early and ask if they could sit in the room with me. A condition of being allowed down early was that they would join in with my prayer time (their alternative was to read a book in bed until it was time to get up).

These simple routines have acted as memorials for our children that they will look back on in years to come, and which will help them on their journey of faith. In our home we have chosen to not only point to God by the things we place on the walls and the things we do, but also to keep a record of what God has done for us as a family.

Keeping a record

God is in the business of answering prayer. Our God is active in our lives and we have many stories of God's goodness to us. Just like the Israelites, it is easy to forget the things God has done for us. We want to keep a record of these things so that we can remind ourselves and tell our children of God at work in our lives.

Some families may choose to keep a memory box containing objects that point to God's clear intervention in their lives. We are not that creative, but we do keep a simple record on a computer.

There we can read of our eldest son's first clear answer to prayer. He was four years old at the time and he had picked up on his parents' less-than-godly complaining. Our trash had not been collected from our house for several weeks in a row, in spite of many phone calls to the council. Every Friday the council would come and collect the rubbish belonging to our neighbors, but every Friday they would leave ours behind.

I'm not sure whether it was an act of faith or a measure of his frustration, but our eldest son prayed on Tuesday evening, "Lord, please let them collect our rubbish tomorrow." The next day the council arrived to remove it.

Some may call this coincidence, but we could see the hand of God at work. On that same list we have stories of God's grace to us and His supernatural provision and healing. One of our children leapt off a playhouse and banged his head. When we got to him his eyes were rolling back and he was going unconscious. We carried him inside and prayed for him. Instantly he sat up, alert and remained well. This incident had to be recorded.

On a different evening, another of our sons came downstairs complaining that he couldn't sleep because his nose was sore. We could see the redness under his nose, resulting from several days of having a cold. We prayed for him, not filled with faith but more as a pacifier to get him back to bed, and instantly the sore skin around his nose transformed before our eyes and became normal. That too had to be placed in our record book.

At the time we thought, "We'll never forget that happening," but of course, over time we forget.

Our children said some very cute things when they were first learning to speak and we thought then that we would never forget them, but we have definitely forgotten most of them. We still remember a few, like the time one of them was screaming in hysterics as we took him to hospital for an injection. He was crying, "I don't want an infection, I don't want an infection!" When we finally worked out that he meant "injection", it was hard for us to keep a straight face. If only we had kept a better record to remember more of these moments.

When we record God at work, it builds our faith. If a problem comes our way, we can point to the record and say we have seen God's faithfulness in our family in the past, so we know that God will continue to be faithful. We may not immediately see the way out of this particular problem, but we can rest assured that it hasn't taken God by surprise, so we can trust that He has a plan.

Every so often our family loves to sit around and tell the stories of what God has done. These stories may be our own experiences, or those of the guests who are with us. Either way they are part of God's story in the world today and these stories are woven into the faith fabric of our children's lives.

Every Jewish family loves to tell a good story – and what better stories are there to tell than those of God at work in our lives?

We are called to remember what God has done, but this is something we have to be very intentional about. I shudder when I see the short memories of the Israelites, soon after they have left Egypt. Instead of trusting God they cried, "We should return to Egypt, life was better there" (Numbers 14:4). They had seen God send plagues, part the sea and provide food supernaturally, yet still they chose to complain rather than trust God. I know this tendency is in me too, so it's good to choose to be intentional in remembering what God has done.

THOUGHTS TO PONDER

1. What memorial objects do you have in your house right now?
2. What have you seen God do in your life and through your life?
3. Do your children know these stories?
4. What can you do in your home to keep these memories alive.

Thank you, God, that You have been faithful to me and my family in the past.

May we continually remember Your goodness to us as a family.

May today's display of Your grace become tomorrow's stepping stone of faith and trust in You, for every member of my family.

Then He spoke to the children of Israel, saying, 'When your children ask their fathers in time to come, saying, "What are these stones?" then you shall let your children know, saying, "Israel crossed over this Jordan on dry land."'
(Joshua 4:21–22)

6

MEMORIAL FESTIVALS

Memories

My brother and I would race each other downstairs each morning. We wanted to be the first to collect the milk from the doorstep, because whoever came first would be the one to open the milk and pour the thick cream, that had risen to the top, on our breakfast cereal. There was nothing better!

Then, when it was Christmastime, we would rush downstairs to see what presents had appeared under the tree. We didn't plan to open any just yet, we just wanted to make sure they were there and try to guess what might be inside.

Then came the waiting time. How early was too early to wake our parents? As soon as they were awake, or at least resembling some form of wakefulness, we would choose a present to open. Invariably this would lead to some kind of construction project taking place in my parents' bedroom while they looked on with sleepy pleasure.

Then Christmas day would continue. It usually involved eating too much food, including various deserts. Then we would wait a couple of hours before eating more desert!

These repeated customs formed the memories of my home. Most homes hold their own unique rituals and traditions that shaped our childhood.

This concept of celebrating feasts together was instituted by God Himself. The feast of Passover, intended to celebrate and recall Israel's release from slavery, began whilst they were still in slavery.

Can you imagine what the second Passover must have looked like? Think of the excitement on their faces as they retold the story of how God had delivered them. What about the first Passover in the Promised Land, when the children who had left Egypt as slaves now passed on this story to their children and encouraged them to do the same? This feast has continued right up to the present day, and is still celebrated, even by more secular Jews.

These feasts are part of the process of creating memories, sharing stories and passing on knowledge of the character of our God.

Celebrating God in the home

Everyone loves a good party – especially those times when school is not on, the parents are home from work, and we have a reason to celebrate. Whether it's a birthday or Christmas we love to build memories together. In the same way, the Jewish people celebrated various feasts together.

Each one of the Jewish feasts has a different emphasis, carries a different thought and reveals a different aspect of God's character. Each allows for the forming of traditions centered on God, which bring Him into the center of the home. God initiated these feasts for the benefit of the Jews and all who follow them.

The Jewish feasts have strong messages and routines that point to Jesus. Colossians 2:16–17 says, "So let no one judge you in food or in drink, or regarding a festival or a new moon or sabbaths, which are a shadow of things to come, but the substance is of Christ." In other words, all the feasts are a shadow of Christ.

Passover reminds us that Jesus has become our Passover Lamb and that we are now no longer slaves to sin.

The Festival of Weeks (Shavuot) celebrates the start of the second harvest in the year. We know this festival by the name Pentecost, when God sent His Holy Spirit to help the Church bring in the end-time harvest of souls for the kingdom. For the Jews this feast is also the time when they remember the giving of the commandments to Moses on Mount Sinai. So, the feast that Christians commemorate to remember the coming of the Holy Spirit, is also the feast that Jews use to commemorate the giving of God's Word. This is a great reminder that we need both the Word of God and the Spirit of God to live fully for God here on earth.

The Feast of Tabernacles (also called Shelters or Sukkoth) marks the end of the harvesttime. The Jews build a shelter and eat under it for a whole week. This reminds them of the time when their ancestors lived in the desert after they had left Egypt. But it is not just a reminder, it is a chance to experience what it is like to continually be in a tent to eat. Scholars believe that Jesus was born in the feast of Tabernacles (when the word became flesh and lived/tabernacle among us). For us as Christians, this feast also reminds us that life on earth is temporary and that Jesus is coming back soon. Because there is so much significance in the Jewish feasts God initiated in the Old Testament, some Christians choose to celebrate these in their homes.

We also try to look out for people in our church community who may be on their own whilst families are celebrating. God says that He sets the lonely in families and we have a family that others can be a part of. Bringing others into our home not only benefits those who would be on their own, but is a great testimony to our children to look out for others.

Whatever way you choose to celebrate God at home, here are some principles you can apply to these celebrations.

Fun, fun, fun

Firstly, they should be fun! Okay, I know family gatherings have a reputation for being stressful and it may be that this is your experience, but having fun together as a family is an important part of living life to the full. If you keep the perspective that the family is the most important part of the celebration, most of the stresses disappear.

So, when the roast dinner you have been preparing for the past three days drops onto the floor as you carry it to the table, you have a choice. You can either burst into tears and storm up to your room, where you replay the incident in your mind for the next two hours as the rest of the family sinks into an awkward silence, or you can burst out laughing and eat cheese on toast instead.

Whatever you do, this day will be remembered. If the adults in the room keep their cool, the children will look back with fondness at the day when the food flopped onto the floor. The aim is not perfection in the details, but joy in each other's company.

Now it may be that one member of the family does not want to share your festive cheer and chooses to moan and complain. You can do your best to decide together what games you will play or what activities you will do, so that every family member feels there is something for them, but ultimately you are not in control of when your toddler, or your teen, or even one of the adults, is having a tantrum. You are in control of how you respond.

Traditions

Many festivals have a rhythm and a routine to them which allow space for good years and bad years, blips and bumps, over the course of years and decades. These repeated routines become something to look forward to and something around which everything else happens.

Traditions may sound old fashioned, and in some cases they are, but they can also be unique to your family. As you celebrate different festivals together as a family, you are building up your children's store of memories. They will be able to look back and say, "Do you remember how we used to …?"

In our family we have a tradition at Christmastime of hiding one present from each child and giving them a clue to help them find it. The older they get, the more cryptic the clues become. This tradition has become something they all look forward to – so much so, that they have started hiding the presents they give to each other, to allow their siblings the joy of hunting out another present.

As traditions are repeated each year the children are filled with excitement. On a number of occasions our children have declared, "Oh, I remember doing this last year." Each time this is said it is with an air of excitement and familiarity, as they connect happy memories from times gone by to the present.

Traditions can relate to the type of food that you eat, the activities you do together, or a specific event that happens at a certain time each day. Traditions may have been passed down from previous generations, or you may be forging a new path for your future family that will be copied for generations to come. Each of the traditions we build in our home reinforce the uniqueness of our family.

Stories

A third part of making memories is the telling of stories. The most obvious stories that will be told are those that relate to the festival you are celebrating. At Easter time you can tell the crucifixion and resurrection story. At Pentecost you can read about the coming of the Holy Spirit. At Christmastime you can track the path of Jesus in the first part of His life on earth. These stories have been shared for generations and all point to God.

How you tell the stories will, of course, be up to you. Will you read the story straight from the Bible? Will you act out the story together as one person narrates it? Will you create crafts to retell the story? Will you try to imagine what an updated version of the story might look like if it took place today? Or maybe you will go the extra mile and create a video of the story in advance to sit around and watch together?

However you choose to tell the story, it is important that you tell it together. Be involved together in the storytelling. If you choose to make a movie, the children might choose to be the actors, or they may help you to create the story using Lego bricks. By taking a series of photographs and piecing them together you will be able to create a stop-motion movie.

The retelling of stories together is an opportunity to share in the emotions and the fun of the moment.

As well as retelling *the* stories related to the festival, take time to tell stories from your past. Tell the funny stories, the family stories and the God stories.

Sitting around the dinner table, we often tell the stories of things God has done for us as a family. We remember the specific prayers that God has answered and the times when everything had gone wrong. These stories become part of our heritage to our children and help to form their identity.

God

All of these traditions and sharing help us to bring God into the festivals. We want our children to have moments in the home where they can encounter God. It might be that we give space for God to speak to them, or for them to reflect on the past year. It might be that they join us to pray into the year ahead, or to thank God for times past.

Whatever way it happens, we want our children to engage with God and to delight in Him. After all, these festivals are not only celebrations, they are opportunities to remember God's faithfulness and to draw closer to Him.

This may seem obvious, but it can be easy to be caught up in the more secular aspects of a celebration and forget who the celebrations are all about. It is good to reflect on how these annual celebrations evolve to make sure that God is at the very center of them.

Remember, every festival should be full of food, fun and faith.

THOUGHTS TO PONDER

1. What festivals do you celebrate together?
2. How do you have fun as a family?
3. What traditions are you developing as a family?
4. What stories of God have been passed down through your generations?

Thank you, Lord that we can celebrate you as a family!

May our homes be full of food, fun and faith as we celebrate the festivals.

"Remember now your Creator in the days of your youth, before the difficult days come, and the years draw near when you say, 'I have no pleasure in them.'"

(Ecclesiastes 12:1)

7

READY FOR MEAT

Children can cope with the Bible!

The Bible is such an important book. In the Jewish family, the children will be raised to read the Torah from a very young age, because they know it is the very foundation of their faith. In our homes too, the Bible is the most important book that our children can live by. We can be tempted to dilute the message of the Bible, in case it is too much for our children to cope with, but as they grow older they will need to hear what the Bible has to say.

> "*Moses commanded them, saying: 'At the end of every seven years, at the appointed time in the year of release, at the Feast of Tabernacles, when all Israel comes to appear before the Lord your God in the place which He chooses, you shall read this law before all Israel in their hearing.'*"
>
> Deuteronomy 31:10–11

In other words, Moses told the people to come together every seven years to read the books of the Law – the first five books of our Bible. These tend to be the books that we avoid reading with our children, especially Leviticus, Numbers and Deuteronomy, as they have less stories and many laws. Yet, every seven years Moses told the people to read them publicly. Moses continues:

> "*Gather the people together, men and women and little ones, and the stranger who is within your gates, that they may hear and that they may learn to fear the Lord your God and carefully observe all the words of this law, and **that their children, who have not known it, may hear and learn to fear the Lord your God as long as you live in the land** which you cross the Jordan to possess.*"
>
> Deuteronomy 31:12–13

69

Did you get that? Moses tells the Israelites to read Leviticus and Deuteronomy out loud to the children, not as some test of endurance, but so that they will learn to fear the Lord. The children were expected to be there for the reading of some of the hardest books of the Bible.

This is not really the model of modern mission. I have not seen any posters advertising public readings of the book of Numbers for a primary school holiday club. Nor am I advocating that it should be happening! All I am pointing out is that God, through Moses, knew that the children of Israel had the spiritual capacity to listen and learn from a reading of the Bible, hearing it twice in the first 14 years of life.

Children can not only cope with the Bible, it is essential for their spiritual growth.

Milk or meat?

Our children need to be fed the meat of God's Word. As they enjoy hearing the stories of God at work through the Bible, it is an introduction to who God is. After 12 years of hearing about God, our children should know enough to be able to pass these truths on to others.

The writer of Hebrews put it this way:

> *"For though by this time you ought to be teachers, you need someone to teach you again the first principles of the oracles of God; and you have come to need milk and not solid food."*

Hebrews 5:12

Moving beyond 'milk teachings' is vital if our children are going to be able to live for God in an age that is rapidly rejecting Him. The next verse of Hebrews says, "But solid food belongs to those who are of full age, that is, those who by reason of use have their senses exercised to discern both good and evil." The phrase "of full age" is not referring to numerical age, but reaching a place of spiritual maturity. In other words, those who can feast on the meat of God's Word are spiritually mature and will be able to discern between good and evil.

To put it the opposite way, a failure to teach the Word of God to our children will lead to a spiritual famine, where they will no longer be able to discern between good and evil.

Today, we are keen to make children's experience of God and church enjoyable, and many resources have been produced to help children access the Bible. In some ways our job has never been easier. Yet, at the same time, we can feel like we have to compete with the messages of the world, which have become slicker in their marketing. Therefore, we can be in danger of dumbing down our spiritual principles, so that our children are left with fragments of truth rather than encounters with the Truth.

The Gospel still has the power to change lives and the more of it our children can read and absorb, the stronger their lives will be. Yet, knowledge of the Bible and its stories is diminishing among our children as Christian values are under threat in the West in a way they have not been in recent history. At such a time our children need to know more of God's Word, not less.

This is something we have to review regularly. Just recently, our eldest son said to us that he felt we were targeting our Bible family times at the youngest members of the family and he wasn't really getting anything from it. In response, we moved from retelling Bible stories to studying the book of Romans. It took us half an hour to get through the first verse as we dug deeply into it together. Our oldest son loved it. More surprisingly, our other children also engaged with it.

When you see the list of "milk topics" described in Hebrews 6:1-3 and compare them with the average teaching we give our children, it's easy to see just how milky their spiritual diet can be:

- Repentance from dead works
- Faith toward God
- The doctrine of baptisms
- Laying on of hands
- Resurrection of the dead
- Eternal judgment

Our children need to know the story of God, but we also have the privilege of helping them to understand the doctrines of God.

A baby who is a few months old can eat meat if it is processed in a food processor. In the same way we can teach the Word of God to our children if we break it up into small enough pieces for them to grab hold of. Children can cope with surprisingly sophisticated topics when it is explained to them simply.

We were recently taking a group of children on a trip through the whole Bible, from Genesis to Revelation, in two days as part of a Bible Experience. When we started speaking about the bowls of God's wrath from Revelation, we told the children how God longs for people to turn to Him, but Revelation 16:9–11 tells us that even though these disasters happen, people won't turn to God but will curse Him instead.

As we taught this, one child piped up, "Like in Egypt."

I was puzzled for a moment as I tried to remember every reference to Egypt in the news that week. Finally, the penny dropped. He was thinking back to the teaching the day before, when we spoke about how Pharaoh had responded to the plagues that God had sent in Moses' time. That child, and all of us in the room, understood the mercy of God at a deeper level that day.

Loving the Scriptures

We don't want to torture our children with the Scriptures; we want them to develop a love for the Scriptures. Our children will be watching how we handle the Bible. We can help them to see how we use verses from the Bible to guide our everyday lives and decisions. When they see this in our lives, they will be more willing to apply Scripture to their own lives.

Jewish families instill such a love for the Tanakh (our Old Testament) in their children, by regular readings and looking to it for instructions.

In times past in the church, reading from the Bible as a whole family was a daily occurrence. Looking back a hundred years, Robert Murray M'Cheyne wrote a Bible reading plan to help people read through the whole Bible in a year. In it, he indicated four chapters to be read every single day. Two of these chapters were intended for personal study and two were intended to be read as a whole family.

We can be sure that not every family in his church read two chapters a day together, however M'Cheyene set this as a challenge, so it was something many families would have aspired to. This regular exposure to Scripture would impact the lives of future generations as they grew in their knowledge of the Bible.

As I travel around, I am privileged to speak to many different people from different backgrounds. Some of the people I most love to talk to are those who were raised in a Christian home and are now in their eighties. These people have a faith that has been refined over decades of serving Jesus and building His kingdom.

As I speak to them, I ask what their memories are of growing up in a Christian home. So far not one person has mentioned the amazing church they went to as a child. Some have mentioned the key influence of a member of the church. Others talked about how their parents' love of God rubbed off on them. Some described how their parents invited many people to share Sunday lunch with them and that became a focal point for talking about Jesus. Many different aspects influenced different individuals in their faith journey, but there was one aspect that they all shared.

Every single one of them has mentioned how the Bible was read every day in their home.

One gentleman said how they would read a chapter from Proverbs in the morning. The chapter they read matched the date: on the first of the month they read Proverbs 1, on the 4th Proverbs 4, and so on. Then, in the evening, his father would take out the King James Version and they would read a passage from the New Testament. To this day, he can still remember the first day he was allowed to read a verse from the family Bible, as a young boy.

Other families followed different patterns of reading, sometimes including discussions on the passage, other times just following a simple reading plan.

You may be reading this thinking, "I don't know if I can even read two verses a day, let alone two chapters." If you do not already read some of the Bible on a regular basis with your family, I want to encourage you to start somewhere. It may be that you choose to celebrate a special meal once a week as a family and, during that time, you read a few verses from the Scriptures. This can be built into your weekly rhythm as a family.

When God reveals something fresh to me from the Bible, I love to share it first with my family. Many a sermon began in my private time with the Lord and was developed in front of my family. If there is a passage of Scripture that God has burned in your heart, share it with your family and tell them what has impacted you about it. Your children will pick up not just the words you are saying, but the passion with which you say them. All of this will help them to grow in their love of Scripture.

Raised in this environment, our son Benjamin chose to read through the whole Bible when he was seven. Having read it through he enjoyed it so much he started to read it through again and again. His love for the Bible knowledge is such that he sees deep insights into God's Word that encourages adults.

It may be that you encourage your children to read a passage from the Bible by themselves on a regular basis. It may be that you follow a theme as a family, to see what God is saying to you collectively. Or you may take it in turns to read from the Bible; or you read a verse each; or you read through the Psalms; or a letter, or the Gospels or Proverbs. Whatever you do, include the reading of Scripture in your routine.

Some families are so busy that they have had to find more creative ways to introduce the Bible into the home. One family selects a Bible verse for the week and puts it up by the door for everyone to read as they leave the house in the morning. Others choose a passage for the week and leave the Bible lying around the house for people, or print out copies of the week's passage to put next to beds, on the fridge and in bags. They then encourage each other to read the story and discuss what God may be saying to their family through it during a weekly time of reflection.

Every family is different, and your family routine will look different to everyone else's, but the principle of the importance of reading, studying and sharing from God's Word together cannot be overstated. Our children are ready for meat, let's not leave them spiritually hungry.

THOUGHTS TO PONDER

1. Do you have times when you read and discuss the Bible as a family?
2. How would you like to develop your Bible reading programme as a family?
3. Are your children hungry for God's Word? Are they well-fed or so hungry they can't even see their need for it?
4. What can you do to help your children grow in their love for the Bible?

Thank you, Lord, for your Bible, the Word of God.

Thank you that the Word did not just stay as a book, but lived as Jesus on the earth.

Help my family grow more in love with the Word and to know the Word more.

"Your Word is a lamp to my feet and a light to my path."

(Psalm 119:105)

8

ACTIVE PARTICIPANTS

Hitting the target

Psalm 127 describes children as arrows in the hands of a warrior. It continues, "…happy is the man who has his quiver full of them." Firstly, note how this verse is addressed to parents. The day we become a parent we become warriors fighting for our children. Secondly, notice how our children are not supposed to be left in the quiver, waiting until they are ready to be used. They are supposed to be in our hands, fired at a target.

The Jews often joke about the role of the Jewish Mama in deciding the future of her children. "You can be whatever you want, as long as it's a Doctor."

Or the more ludicrous Jewish joke:

> The United States of America has recently elected its first Jewish President and it is the day of his inauguration. In the front row sits the new President's mother, who leans over to a senator sitting next to her.
> "You see that man over there with his hand on the Bible?"
> "Yes I do," the Senator whispers back.
> His mother proudly says, "His brother's a doctor."

When we talk about 'targeting' our children for the future, I am not saying we should set our hearts on a specific profession or plan an arranged marriage for them. It is not a case of, "We have your whole life mapped out for you, so you have no freedom to choose what you want for your life." If such specifics are not the target for our children, then what is?

- Do we want them to fulfil God's call on their life?

- Do we want them to grow up to be good citizens in society?

- Do we want them to have a good knowledge of the Bible?

- Do we want them to have a heart for the needy and marginalized of society?
- Do we want them to hear and obey when God speaks to them?
- Do we want them to exhibit the character of Jesus in every circumstance?
- Do we want them to move in the power of God?
- Do we want them to be influencers for good with everyone they meet?

The answer to all these questions is probably a resounding "Yes!" All of these are characteristics we would like to see in our children. The problem is, they cannot all be the target. When you fire an arrow, you have to aim for one (and only one) specific spot. You cannot fire an arrow effectively if you are trying to aim in eight different places at the same time.

So, what is the one target?

I would suggest that the target is Jesus. When our children encounter Jesus, they become the best version of who they are called to be. When they encounter Jesus, they want to study the Bible to learn more about Him. Meeting Jesus gives them a heart for the poor and needy and a desire for more of God's power, so that they can meet those needs. Meeting Jesus gives them the confidence to be the same person, no matter where they go, meaning they will be influencers for good. Meeting Jesus helps them to see the world from God's perspective.

One girl said, "When I found out most people in my class were on a WhatsApp group, but had left out the class loner, I added her. She came and thanked me for including her in the group."

Following a weekend away with his church, one boy commented, "When I went back to school everything was different. It was like everyone else had met with Jesus too."

A teenage girl was at a party when someone suggested a game that involved the boys lying on top of the girls. This girl said bluntly, "I am not going to play that." Because of her courage to speak up, several other girls also opted out.

A young boy on his first sleepover listened as everyone else suggested they play a game of 'Truth or Dare' (a game that involves being dared to do something silly or sharing a truth you don't want to share). He saw that it could end badly and said, "I don't want to play that, let's do this instead." Everyone followed his lead.

An encounter with Jesus transforms hearts and leads to right actions. As we build rhythm and ritual into our children's lives we are giving them multiple opportunities to discover, engage with and be transformed by God. Our children are not supposed to be 'spectators' of these things as we perform them in front of them – God wants them to actively participate in the rhythm and rituals in the home.

Jewish tradition expects this kind of engagement from children. Children are allowed to be active participants in the expression of faith within the home. From asking questions to helping retell stories, children are at the heart of the faith life in the home.

Personal devotions

As well as our communal times with the God, we want our children to develop their own personal relationship with Him. To talk with and to get to know God as a child is the greatest gift we can give our children to prepare them for their future.

Part of this process includes encouraging our children to have their own personal devotional times. To begin with, we encourage our children to pray each day for as many minutes as they are years old: a six-year-old prays for six minutes a day, and a ten-year-old prays for ten minutes a day. This gradual growth of time with the Lord makes prayer a reflex for them. In our home we encourage this from the age of five.

For children who need a bit of help with what to do during this time, we suggest using the STOP prayer (Sorry-Thankyou-Others-Please). Children can pray through each of these steps and then remember to STOP and listen to God by reading the Bible and taking time to listen to what the Holy Spirit wants to show them.

I know some parents who feel reluctant to encourage their children to do this, as they do not want to force them. But, as parents we are willing to encourage our children to do other things that they don't yet see the value of, because we know they are good for them. For example, we make space in the day for them to brush their teeth and stay with them while they perfect their technique. In the same way we can encourage our children to spend time with God. Of course, there is a big difference between actively encouraging and aggressively forcing our children to do something. But we should not let the fear of the latter (which is clearly counterproductive for their spiritual growth) stop us from doing the former. After a few months of building personal devotional times into the rhythm of our family life, they became the norm.

Are you listening?

One key aspect of connecting with God is to allow our children to hear God speaking to them.

Each child is a unique individual. Each one hears God in their own way. So, while there is no one-size-fits-all way of hearing from God, there are a number of things we can do to help our children to hear Him.

Firstly, we can talk with them about how God speaks to us. The most important way God speaks is through the Bible. This is God's unchanging Word to the world. But, this is not the only way God speaks. The Bible itself shows us that God can speak to us in an audible voice, through a donkey, as an inner prompting, a vision, a dream, through other believers and through all of creation (which is busy declaring the glory of God). God communicates in many varied ways and different people will hear God speaking to them in different ways, during different seasons of their lives.

Secondly, we can talk about our experience of God speaking to us. We will have those moments when a Bible verse leapt off the page and helped us with a particular situation, such as knowing how to respond to someone we were struggling with at work. Perhaps there was a time when we had a feeling about not doing something and it turned out that feeling was from God. Or a God-idea that we decided to try, even though we were not 100% sure it was God, but which proved to be from Him when we looked back on it. Or that inner voice when God spoke something specifically to us.

Back in the days when many ministers wore suits and ties, I was a young children's pastor. Feeling discouraged in the ministry, I went to God and asked Him what I could do to be more effective. I heard God speak in my mind, saying, "Wear a suit on Sundays." Now, I admit that suits are not the normal attire for children's ministers, but I thought I would roll with it.

That first Sunday, I walked into the church and the children's eyes lit up. "Now we have a proper pastor," I heard one young child say and the others sat up more. That one action helped them to feel more valued members of the church. Parents also treated me differently, feeling safer with confiding in me. The ministry became more effective to the whole family and all because I did something simple based on a word from God.

Thirdly, we can teach them what to expect when God speaks to them. The apostle Paul sought to be led by the Spirit in everyday life. In Acts 16:6 he speaks of how the Spirit stopped him from going to Asia, because God had other plans for him. We want our children to enjoy this same blessing of being led by the Holy Spirit. While acknowledging that God will speak to us in different ways, we have found it helpful to talk to children about what it is like when God speaks.

When we spend time in God's presence, He often speaks into our imagination using words and pictures. Of course, this is not a fool-proof method of hearing God speak, as it could simply be our own imaginings, but when we are in God's presence, His thoughts more readily become our thoughts.

Over time children learn to recognize when a thought in their head is from God and when it is just from their imagination. A good understanding of the nature of God, as revealed in the Bible, will also help children to discern what is from God and what isn't.

Fourthly, give space for God to speak and children to grow. Once children know what to expect, we can give them space to hear from God, for example during a time of family devotion. To begin with your child may hear nothing, or they may hear that you are going to take them to their favorite restaurant for the day! Admittedly, this may not be God speaking, but do not be discouraged. In every other area of child development we are willing to give our children time to get the hang of things and this should be no different.

When a baby first makes incoherent noises, we don't say, "That's not a proper word. Until you can speak properly don't make another sound." No, we understand that this is part of them getting used to the idea of making noises, until one day they say, "Da!" At that moment, tears well up in our eyes and we repeat, "Yes, Da. That's Daddy." We announce it on social media, call the grandparents and book their place in a prestigious university, all within the next hour. (Unfortunately, we discover that they don't seem to repeat this when we want to show their newfound skill to visitors!) Our baby learns from our feedback and their experience, while they are immersed in an environment of speech.

When it comes to walking, we don't force a crawling child to stay still until they can walk properly. Instead, we encourage all movement and rejoice over the small steps they take, even though they stumble. Our toddler grows in an environment where we believe in them and encourage them to keep trying.

When a child comes home from school, struggling with their homework, we don't tell them to quit and suggest they go out and find a menial job to do for the rest of their life. Instead we support them in their discouragement and encourage them to have another go.

In short, we gave space for our children to succeed on a regular basis. Space enough that they may actually fail, but if they do fail we don't call this failure a dead-end, rather a stepping stone to becoming the great person God has called them to be.

In the same way we can give them space to hear from God. Often the first word a child hears from God is, "I love you." Three more powerful words you will not find. An understanding of God's unconditional love is enough to carry us through every future season of life. This is a cause for celebration. At the same time, the first words children hear can be deeply profound, even if it takes a while to come.

When Matthew, our middle son, was around four years old he spoke up for the first time in our family devotions. We had given space for God to speak to us and Matthew chirped in saying, "God says I'm a face." After much puzzling we had absolutely no clue whether this word had any real meaning, or even if it was from God, but we smiled at his attempts to be a part of things.

The next day Matthew heard the same words again. And the following day. And the day after that.

"He always says that," his older brother cried. "That's not God, he's just making it up."

"It's fine. Give him space," we replied.

And so we did. Day after day, week after week, Matthew repeated this phrase. One month passed, then two, then three, and each day Matthew would speak out these mysterious words: "God says I'm a face."

Six months passed and Matthew was still going, until one day he said something different: "Daddy in France. Man lying down, glass shatters. Daddy turns left." At the time I was ministering in a Bible school in France. This part of what Matthew said was not prophetic, we had told him where I had gone. The rest of it did not make sense, but my wife, using her grand discernment, realized that for the first time in six months Matthew had said something different to, "I'm a face." So, she texted the word to me.

As I looked at the word, the pastor of the college came over and started to read it too. "This word is amazing!" he exclaimed. "There is a recognized national prophet in France who has said that the church is like a man lying down over the map of France, pressed down by a sheet of ice. But the ice suddenly shatters and the church is able to rise up."

"Daddy in France. Man lying down, glass shatters."

My son's first prophetic word that we understood was a word for a whole nation that matched the word of a recognized prophet (even if it was delivered at a four-year-old level of speaking).

When it came to the last bit of his message, "Daddy turns left," we weren't to clear what this meant, but around this time we started to connect with a minister called Roberts Liardon. We have now co-authored many books together as part of the *God's Generals for Kids* series. These books are one of the most significant aspects of my ministry so far. If you start at Marseille, in the South of France and turn left, drifting slightly south as you go, you come to Florida where Roberts Liardon lives.

In other words, my son's first recognizable word was a word for a whole nation and a significant confirmation of the future direction of our ministry. But before this word we had to endure six months of, "God says I'm a face."

Several years on and Matthew has grown in his ability to hear God speaking, as we have continued to make space for Him to speak to us through His Word and by His Spirit.

Let's make space to help our children hear from God, so that they will be ready to step out and obey Him. You can read many stories of children and young people hearing from God in our book *The Josiah Generation*.

Hearing from God is not the endpoint of discipleship. Having heard God, we need to obey Him.

THOUGHTS TO PONDER

1. How do your children engage with God at home?
2. Do you make space for them to hear God speaking to them?
3. What challenges do you have (or anticipate having) to encourage your children in times of daily devotion?
4. How can you overcome these challenges?

Lord, I want my children to have an active relationship with you.

I do not want them to be spectators of the Christian faith, but to be active participants.

Meet with my children and set their hearts on fire to live for you.

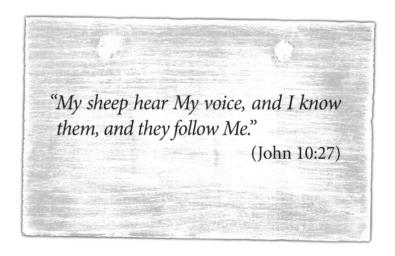

"My sheep hear My voice, and I know them, and they follow Me."
(John 10:27)

At home with God

9

INVOLVE THE CHILDREN

God is inclusive

In Chapter Six I spoke about the importance of retelling stories in the home. These stories are opportunities to involve children as they learn. Our faith is not something we do to them, it is something we share together. Involving our children is not a token gesture, but an acknowledgment that children can be full members of the Body of Christ.

Children are ready to start playing their part in the church today. The prayers they pray are not practice prayers, they are the real thing. Their worship glorifies God. They can grow in godly character. They have a part to play in God's kingdom, now and in their future.

In Ephesians 5:21–6:10 the apostle Paul writes to the church in Ephesus. At the time he was stuck in prison and likely dictated the letter while a scribe wrote it down. This letter was then carried to the church in Ephesus, which met in homes around the city, where it would have been read aloud in each of the congregations who gathered together.

In this passage Paul addresses wives, husbands, children, fathers, slaves and masters. Interestingly, Paul speaks directly to the children in Ephesians 6:1: "Children, obey your parents…" He could have put across the same message by saying, "Parents, make sure your children obey you…" This would have been in line with the principle of parents being the primary disciplers of their children. Yet Paul addressed his words to the children. He expected them to be there and to be listening as this part of the letter was read out.

Ephesians 5:34 says, "Now hurry and gather your children from the next-door room. Quickly tell them to put down their coloring books and electronic devices, for the next verse is for them." Then in Ephesians 6:3½ you will read, "Now children, you may go back to playing, the rest of the letter is irrelevant for you."

Okay, so those two verses don't actually exist! There is no cue to tell the children to come and listen to the teaching; the children were present throughout. So, when Paul says in Ephesians 6:10, "Finally, my brethren…" he is speaking to the *whole* of the church. For the early Church it would have been no surprise that children were included in their gathering – the biggest shock was that slaves and masters could sit together in the same room as equals. In our modern culture, a boss and his employee can attend the same church, but children can often be relegated to second place. Even our terminology can reinforce this. For example, does your church refer to the adult meeting as the 'main service'? This can send out the message that the kids and youth groups are not the 'main thing', but of secondary importance.

Frequently children would have been included in biblical events because their families were there. We don't know how many children and youth were present in the upper room when the Holy Spirit came at Pentecost. Some of the apostles may still been teenagers at this point. Though the Bible doesn't tell us the ages of those in the upper room, it most certainly doesn't exclude children. In a culture where children were part of whatever was going on, the balance of probability is that some children would have been present; and if they were, then they would have been receiving the Holy Spirit on the day of Pentecost too.

In our homes we want our children to encounter God for themselves. Though we may have known God for more years than they have been alive, they will almost certainly have a more childlike relationship with God than we do. Their growth with God can inspire our growth, as we learn from each other.

Salt and light

Whether you have a daily or weekly rhythm for family times, and whether your focus is around a meal or part of the bedtime routine, make space for your children to connect with God at home. As they encounter God for themselves at home, you can encourage them to live for God wherever they go.

Jesus said, in Matthew 5:13, "You are the salt of the earth," and in Matthew 5:14, "You are the light of the world." Jesus does not say "You will *become*" salt and light, He says we are them already. Neither does He ask the question, "*Will you be* the salt/light?" It is simply a question of whether we are being effective in the world as salt, and whether we are letting our light shine.

This is true for you and me, but any person who is following God – regardless of their age – is salt and light to this world. The question is whether they will lose their saltiness and hide their light or put it on display to affect those around them.

When our children are following God, they will want to be active members of the church community and make a stand for Him in their schools. There are many ways we can support them in this. The starting point is to be available to listen to our children.

Within the rhythm and routines of life, if we create an environment where faith and God are not taboo topics or reserved only for special occasions, we will have made a place where our children can flourish. If our children know they can bring any problem to us, without us immediately pouncing on them, they will feel freer to come to us, and we can support them more effectively as they mature.

This involves us connecting with our children at a heart level; being willing to give them time to speak and to listen to what they are saying before we jump in and tell them what to do. Growing this heart connection with our children frees them to grow with God.

When our children take a stand and do the right thing, we should be their greatest supporters. If our children mess up and compromise their values, we should be their greatest encouragers.

When talking to my children about different situations they face, I have found it helpful to hold in my mind a vision of who God is calling them to be, rather than who they are now. This changes the way I speak with them.

Co-ministers

We can also create opportunities for our children to grow in ministry alongside us and in our church communities. If you are involved in a ministry within your church, why not let your children serve and grow alongside you? When we are intentional about including our children in our ministry, we are giving them another opportunity to learn from us in a different context.

Every church has a whole host of activities that need volunteers to keep them going. By allowing our children to volunteer and providing the taxi service to make it possible, we are allowing them to take their place in the community.

From the worship team to the welcome desk, from the creche to the café, there are plenty of places our children can enhance their community. Some aspects of ministry will not be practical for them (toddlers serving boiling tea comes to mind). The younger they are, the more their ministry will be limited to the areas we ourselves are involved in. But, as they grow older, they can find their own niche without us.

When our children work with other members of a team, this builds relationships across the generations. Once again, we are back to doing life together so that everyone benefits. While there can be challenges to including children and young people in church teams, the main challenge is a change of mindset. If children are accepted as part of the Body of Christ, there should be a desire to include them in as many different ways as possible.

One family I know would regularly take their children out onto the streets to hand out flyers. Several months after one such expedition they were stopped by a lady who said, "I was walking past your family one day as you were giving out flyers and I planned to ignore you, but your son was so cute and remarkably persistent that I could not turn him down. When I arrived back home I read the leaflet, joined my local church and have been following God ever since."

The church is a great setting in which children can experiment with praying bold prayers in a safe place, to practice sharing what they feel God is saying to them, and to step out in new branches of ministry. All of this becomes part of the process of equipping our children, so that they can do the same things amongst their non-Christian friends.

Releasing our children in ministry does have some potential dangers. The greatest danger comes if we allow our children to view their service as a performance rather than an act of worship to God. The more gifted they are in a particular area, the greater this danger is.

In a strong church community this can be compounded by members of the congregation offering your children unqualified encouragement. Comments such as, "Well done, you are doing an amazing job" are well meaning, but can build a feeling of "I am amazing!" Even though this is probably true, it can take away from what God is doing through them. For some children it can lead to a focus on *what they do*, and result in the "Martha syndrome" later in life.

An alternative encouragement would be, "Well done, I can see God is really using you." This encourages the child in what they are doing, but keeps the focus on God. When people build my children up, we take extra care to discuss how God was using them as part of the debrief process. Sometimes, when God has moved in a specific or tangible way, we use this opportunity to talk with our children about how God has naturally gifted them to do well in some area of ministry, but when God worked through their natural gifting the impact was astounding.

If your children do join you in ministry, take the opportunity to model to them the process of ministry. Let them be part of praying into the ministry beforehand, highlighting our dependence on God. Take time to debrief them on how they found things afterwards. Highlight to them the things that they did well and the things that God was doing through the team involved in the ministry. Talk through any issues that arose and use these as an opportunity for further discipleship discussion. All of this helps them to become grounded in ministry, keeping the focus on God rather than themselves.

The rewards of such ministry are felt beyond the boundaries of your family. As your children serve alongside other members of the church community, they get to see faith in action in the lives of other believers from a different generation to their own. These relationships often provide great encouragement, both to your children and the rest of the team. Not only that, but you are helping to prepare your children to be active members of the Body of

Christ. This strengthens the intergenerational relationships that are important for the spiritual health of every member of the church.

If your older children help with the children's ministry, they will probably become role models that the younger children can look up to and aspire to be like. After all, the church community is not one-sided and we often benefit more when we give to others, than when we receive from them. When our children step into the role of givers within the church family, they too can benefit greatly. Many a future calling has been stirred up in a child who has been allowed the opportunity to play their part in church.

One mother saw the need for musicians in the church, so she started to invest in music lessons for all five of her children. Now all of them are grown up with families of their own and are involved in the worship ministry in their churches. This kind of proactive approach to releasing our children in ministry will build the future church long after we have gone.

Faith development

When we have a vision for our children as part of the church, we can help them to actively develop their faith. This is something that will happen "accidentally" *if they are in the right environment.* Put another way, if we are intentional about creating the right environment for our children to grow up in, their faith will flourish.

I have to confess that as a family we are not great at keeping plants alive. We know a bit of the theory of horticulture (plants need water and light), but are less good at the practical aspects (keeping them in the right part of the house and remembering to water them!) When a plant is in the right environment it will thrive. Occasionally, some extra intervention is required to combat disease, but mostly it is about making sure its surroundings are right. In the same way, a child placed in the right environment will thrive. When we build a foundation of rituals and rhythms in the home, our children's faith will flourish in other settings too.

As you watch your children grow with the Lord, you will see seasons where they are flourishing with God and seasons where they need to be encouraged. Proactively seek to create the right environment, even if the changes are gradual. This is especially important if your children are disengaging from the spiritual life of the church and home. In the next chapter we will focus specifically on what we can do if our children are disinterested in the things of God.

THOUGHTS TO PONDER

1. Are you involved in a church ministry that your children can be a part of?
2. How can you support them in this ministry?
3. Can you identify the natural giftings on your children's life?
4. How could these gifts be used in the church community?

Lord, help my children to reach their full potential in you.
Help me to release them and not hold them back.
Use our family for your glory wherever we go.

"I press toward the goal for the prize of the upward call of God in Christ Jesus."
(Philippians 3:14)

10

THE RELUCTANT CHILD

So far in this book I have presented some simple scriptural principles that, if applied, can create the right environment for a child's faith to grow. It all seems so neat and tidy when written down. The reality is a lot messier. The theory may sound great, but the practical application of this can be challenging. What do you do if one or more of your children do not want to engage in the awesome plan that you have for their life-changing encounter with God?

We don't want to drag our children kicking and screaming into God's presence. Encountering God is not supposed to be a tortuous affair for the family. Instead of us dragging them to God, we want the Holy Spirit to draw them to Him. So, what can we do if our children seem totally disinterested or even actively opposed to anything to do with God?

The following four steps will help you to keep your family on an even keel in stormy times.

Don't panic

"Help! My child doesn't want anything to do with God at home!"

Firstly, don't panic! If you panic this can lead to irrational, unloving, un-Christlike behavior. If your child is in a season of disinterest, don't picture that season as a life sentence. The life sentence is the call of God on their lives.

Our children (and we ourselves) pass through many different seasons in our walk with God. These seasons do not define them or us. Rather, our children are defined by the life-call that God has placed on their lives and the choices they make. If they are going through a season where they are less interested in the things of God, it is not our job to force them back to Him. Instead, it is our role to support them through this season.

These times don't define our children, but they can help refine them. When we see that God can work in them during this time, we can relax and find God's journey in it all. After all, God wants your child to follow Him even more than you do – and He has put that child in your family for a reason.

Keep to your rhythm

Having said that, this does not mean we cut God out of our family routine. As parents we define our families. As an example of this balance, we don't require our children to pray as part of their bedtime routine, but we do pray for them, because that is who we are as a family. We don't force our children to join in with a worship time, but we do expect them to be present when we worship God, because that is what we do as a family. We don't force our children to attend the children's groups in church, but we do expect them to come to church because that's what we do as a family. In summary, we don't force our children to participate in anything, but we do expect them to attend.

Participation in serving God must come from a person's heart, not because they have been compelled to do it. But our children are naturally "involved" in what we do, because of the nature of our family. As a family, our values are defined by our relationship with God. Our discipline is based on God's standards, and the way we relate to each other is a reflection of our understanding of God's love. In other words, we cannot separate the God-part of our family from the rest of family life.

Having said that, every family functions differently. What counts as "attendance" for one family will be considered overkill for another. However, a strong family rhythm, with God at the center, will be remembered as a place of stability in the future. Don't quit your routine whilst waiting on God to warm their hearts to Him once more.

Show love

During times when our children are doubting, what we do is more significant than what they do. There are things we can proactively do to help our children. If we react out of frustration to a heart that is cold towards God, that can serve to push them further away. If, on the other hand, we continue to show the unconditional love of God (as opposed to conditional love based on whether they follow God or make choices that we agree with) then we are fulfilling the role expected of any decent human being. We are also showing something of Christ to them.

Love is patient; love is kind; it keeps no record of wrongdoing; it is not self-seeking; it is not easily angered. As 1 Corinthians 13:7 says, "love always protects, always trusts, always hopes, always perseveres."

During this time of waiting, continue to bless your children and let God shine through you.

Force don't hope

There is one tool in our armory that is unique to us as Christians and it is effective; a secret weapon that we can wield and that produces results. *Prayer*. With our child we should be gentle and loving, but in prayer we must be forceful.

Jesus put it this way:

> *"And from the days of John the Baptist until now the kingdom of heaven suffers violence, and the violent take it by force."*
>
> Matthew 11:12

The advancing of the kingdom of heaven requires violence – not towards people, but in the spiritual realm. Earlier I quoted from Psalm 127, which speaks about parents as warriors and their children as arrows in their hands. We are called to fight for our children. Nowhere is that fight more important than in the spiritual realm.

Paul said in Ephesians 6:12, "For we do not wrestle against flesh and blood, but against principalities, against powers, against the rulers of the darkness of this age, against spiritual hosts of wickedness in the heavenly places."

Our prayers have the power to change the course of our children's lives. As such, we should not simply sit back and hope that our children return to God – we need to be actively praying for them. As parents this is our duty and our privilege. We cannot expect our church's children's leaders to pray for each of our children individually (especially if they are not facing a crisis). The leadership of the church will probably not be covering our child's specific needs in prayer daily, since they are already carrying many of the congregation in their prayers.

Yet, we are uniquely positioned to know the needs of our children and to have a vested interested in praying for them through the more challenging seasons of life. We can, and indeed should, recruit others to join us in prayer for our children when they are facing a spiritual drought, but the responsibility for all of this lies with us.

I try to make the habit of praying for each of my children for two minutes each day. At times I have needed longer to pray through issues they were facing in their lives. At other times I have prayed everything that comes to mind within the first 10 seconds. This leads to an interesting 1 minute and 50 seconds of praying into things that I would not normally consider: their future spouse and children; their future calling; and for greater revelation from God.

These specific prayers are stored up over their lives, preparing the way for their future. These prayers are not about their future career, but their future relationship with God and their character. If their heart is running after God and they are exhibiting the character of Christ, everything else will fall into place in their lives. The opposite to this is more concerning: they could be successful in every area of their lives, yet be distant from God. Our prayers to God invite Him to step into our children's lives in a life-changing way. As Charles Spurgeon, the famous preacher, said, "Prayer is the slender nerve that moves the muscle of omnipotence."

Through prayer we have seen blasphemers become preachers, convicts become converts, mockers become mouthpieces for the Gospel. Sometimes it seems that the further someone has drifted away, the more dramatic the comeback. Persistent prayer that refuses to accept the status quo brings change. This is the heart of Jesus' teaching on prayer in Luke 11:5–13. Don't stop storming heaven until God breaks in.

Remember, you are not on your own. Ask some of the church community to pray with you for your children. And keep on asking. You can never have too much prayer! If ever you pray for our ministry, please pray for our children's relationship with God to grow continually stronger. We have sometimes intensified prayers for one of our children when we have seen that their hearts are not as passionate for God as they have been in the past. Each time we have seen God reignite something inside of them.

Remember, God gave you your children, knowing that you have what it takes to help them become everything He has called them to be. Don't stop praying until you see God break into their lives.

THOUGHTS TO PONDER

1. What promises has God spoken over their lives so far?
2. Do you trust that God has all things under control?
3. Can you step up your prayers for your child?
4. Who is around you who can support you spiritually as you raise your children?

Lord, teach me to be generous,

to serve you as you deserve,

to give and not to count the cost,

to fight and not to heed the wounds,

to toil and not to seek for rest,

to labor and not to look for any reward,

save that of knowing that I do your holy will.

"Then Jesus told his disciples a parable to show them that they should always pray and not give up."

(Luke 18:1)

The reluctant child

At home with God

PART 3

A GROWING FAITH

11

SPIRITUAL EXPOSURE

Stages of faith

Faith development has been studied by many people, most notably in James Fowler's *Stages of faith* and John Westerhoff's *Will our children have faith?*. When I read about these concepts, based on child development theory, I could see how they related to the children we work with. I couldn't, however, find these stages outlined in the Bible. This sent me on a quest to discover the stages of faith that our children will pass through according to Scripture.

As I studied and prayed, I didn't discover any mention of stages of faith that our children will pass through, but I did find stages of faith that they should be *exposed to*, in order to help with their faith formation. To use the language I used earlier, these 'stages' translate into the different environments our children require at different stages of their growth.

Baby Moses

The first stage of faith, for babies and toddlers, is spiritual exposure. Our youngest children need to be exposed to the presence of God.

When baby Moses was born, his mother hid him away for several months. In an attempt to reduce the growing population of Israelite slaves, the Egyptian Pharaoh had issued a decree that all Israelite baby boys should be killed. Hebrews 11:23 tells us that, "By faith Moses, when he was born, was hidden three months by his parents, because they saw he was a beautiful child; and they were not afraid of the king's command."

This statement is quite ridiculous taken at face value. Few parents look at their newborn baby and say, "This one's not beautiful – they won't amount to much!" Most parents look at their baby through rose-tinted glasses, seeing their unblemished potential. Yet by faith, Moses' parents saw something more. They saw something of God in this child. It was so clear to them that they were willing to risk their own lives to protect him.

After three months Moses was too noisy to be hidden any longer, so Moses' mother made a basket and took him down to the river to leave him there. Her hope was that somebody would walk by, see the baby and have compassion on him. No doubt she also hoped that he wouldn't die of hunger, float off downstream away from the bathing area, capsize, be attacked by wild animals or suffer any other fate!

As she left him and returned to her home, she did not expect to see him again, but trusted that God would take care of her baby. We don't know what she did when she got home, but from what we know of humans in crisis she probably either collapsed in a heap of tears or set about cleaning her house to take her mind off the trauma and carry on with life. Whatever his mother was up to, Moses' sister, Miriam, chose to stay by the river to see what happened.

Before long Pharaoh's daughter arrives on the scene. She sees the baby and immediately feels compassion for him.

"Quick, run and get some formula milk for this poor child."

Her servants look on with confusion.

"But your majesty, they haven't yet invented formula milk yet."

"Then find me a woman who can nurse this child," Pharaoh's daughter orders.

At this moment Miriam pops up from the reeds.

"I know someone who can help, follow me."

And with that she races off towards her home, arriving ahead of Pharaoh's daughter and out of breath.

"Mum, Mum, you are not going to believe this. Our baby is safe. Pharaoh's daughter is going to raise him and she'll be here any minute now."

If Moses' mum wasn't cleaning the house before, she's definitely cleaning now.

Pharaoh's daughter enters the house and casts her eye around the place.

"Woman, will you nurse this child? I will pay you well and you shall come and live in the palace with me, where he shall be raised."

Moses' mother can hardly speak as she nods her head in response. She had given up her child for dead, now she has received him back. What is more, she will be paid to look after him and he will receive the best education Egypt has to offer. This is far more than she could have hoped for.

Day after day, week after week she sits in the luxurious surroundings, taking care of her *own* son. This woman, who by faith had hidden her child, now holds him in her arms without fear of being caught.

The Bible doesn't tell us how she responded, but at the very least she would have thanked God for the life of her son. Perhaps she worshipped God as she held her son in her arms. Maybe she even prophesied over him: "Pharaoh's daughter called you the 'drawn out' one. God will use you to draw His people out of slavery."

Moses was exposed to the presence of God as a baby and that was the start of his calling. Hebrews 11:24–25 says, "By faith Moses, when he became of age, refused to be called the son of Pharaoh's daughter, choosing rather to suffer affliction with the people of God than to enjoy the passing pleasures of sin."

He was willing to reject his upbringing and a life of luxury to associate himself with a bunch of slaves! How did God put this desire into Moses? I would suggest those early years in his mother's arms had a large part to play in preparing him for his future.

Samuel

In the same way, we read that Samuel was exposed to God's presence as a baby. His mother, Hannah, had longed for a baby but had been unable to conceive. One day, when she went up to Jerusalem, she was fasting and crying in desperation for God to give her a child. At this moment she promised and dedicated her first child to God. Eli, the priest, saw her and rebuked her for being drunk. But when she explained that she was not drunk, just desperate, Eli said, "May God grant your request." That year she became pregnant and gave birth to Samuel.

Throughout her pregnancy no doubt Hannah was thinking of the vow she made and telling God, "This baby is yours." How do we know this? Because she kept her vow.

Initially, when her husband invites her to go to Jerusalem for the feast, she refuses to go. "Not until the child is weaned," she replies. "When he is weaned I will take him to the Lord and leave him there." The vow that she has made to the Lord is at the very front of her mind. She plans to follow through on her promise.

So, what would this woman have been doing while she fed her baby? She certainly wasn't flicking through TV channels to find something decent to watch. Nor was she seeking out YouTube videos to entertain herself. Such modern distractions had not yet been invented. Instead, we can assume that because of her commitment to her vow, she was making the most of every moment with her son.

She had struggled with infertility for a long time. Now, however, with the birth of Samuel, the taunts of Elkanah's other wife, the shame of infertility, and the inward struggle of the greatest issue she had ever faced were all removed. She was a woman who was finally free from the greatest trial she had ever faced.

This woman, who had sought God and had her prayers answered, would have been worshipping and thanking God throughout her pregnancy and later as she nursed her son. I have no doubt that she would have reiterated many times her promise that he was dedicated and devoted to the Lord for the whole of his life.

When she finally handed him over to live in the temple a few years later, Samuel entered a very different environment. He left a place of safety and deep love to enter a place where he was isolated from other children. He was in the temple of God. It may sound like the perfect spiritual environment to be raised in, but the reality was far from that.

His foster father was Eli, the High Priest. This man did not have the discernment to be able to tell the difference between a drunk woman and one who was desperate. This man had been unable to raise his own children to a godly standard. Eli's sons were evil in God's sight. They did not value the sacrifices that were made and intimidated people who came to give sacrifices to the Lord. Eli refused to confront or discipline these abusive young men. These were Samuel's foster brothers, his older 'role models.' This is not the environment most parents would choose for their children.

Yet somehow Samuel grew up to be different. God's call was clearly on his life, but God used his godly mother, Hannah, to sow a seed of spiritual connection into his life.

Others

There are many others whose parents would have spoken words of life into their young children and brought them into God's presence through worship and thanksgiving. We can imagine the impact that Samson's parents must have had on him, having seen the angel of the Lord and heard God's planned purpose for his life.

Elizabeth, the mother of John the Baptist, who had been barren, hid herself away when she discovered that she was pregnant. Mary, the mother of Jesus, responded to the angel's announcement of her pregnancy with an echo of the song of praise sung by Hannah, Samuel's mother.

Indeed, any of the godly women of the Bible, whom God gifted with children and informed them of their call, could be expected to have responded with thankfulness, praise and prophetic anticipation for the future of their children. And all of this would have happened in the presence of their children.

In short, these young children were exposed to the presence of the God through the praises of their parents. Even children in the womb can respond to the presence of God. In Luke 1 you can see how John the Baptist responded to Jesus whilst both were in the womb. Many pregnant people have spoken of their babies responding to anointed preaching or worship, where God's presence is tangibly felt. For more about this stage of life see our book, *Jesus, Your Baby and You.*

Young children love the presence of God. In 1905 God poured out His Spirit in a special way in a place called Azusa Street. The Azusa Street Revival was a spectacular outpouring of the power of God. At times, God's presence would manifest itself as flames on the roof of the building where they met and as a physical cloud of His glory inside the building. At these times the greatest miracles took place, and the babies who were in the room would be playing with the cloud of God's glory. There is a natural spiritual hunger among young children for the presence of God.

We used to run a regular meeting in the church for children aged 0–5. In these meetings we would take time to teach the children from God's Word and to praise God together, knowing that their praise was powerful. As it says in Psalm 8:2, "Out of the mouth of babes and nursing infants you have ordained strength, because of Your enemies, that You may silence the enemy and the avenger."

After these meetings many parents would feed back to us that their babies left the place smiling and giggling. They noticed that their children did not want to eat food and were extra smiley for the rest of the day. These children had been impacted by an encounter with God and His peace and joy had filled them.

In our homes we can expose our babies and toddlers to the presence of God as we have times of worship and prayer. We can pray with our children and prophesy over their lives. Through this they will become familiar with the presence of God and desire more of His presence. Even if we are too exhausted to pray, we can put on some worship music in the background as we go about our daily tasks.

All of this is the first stage of faith development we can offer our children, preparing them for when they grow older.

THOUGHTS TO PONDER

1. How are you exposing your babies and toddlers to the presence of God at home?
2. Have you noticed your children engaging with God?
3. What place does worship have in your home?

Lord, let my children encounter you when they are young.
Let them taste and see that you are good.
Let them respond to you in worship.

"Out of the mouth of babes and nursing infants You have ordained strength, because of Your enemies, that You may silence the enemy and the avenger."
(Psalm 8:2)

12

SPIRITUAL EXPERIENCE

God is real

The second phase of faith development that we see in Scripture takes place in children who are above toddler age, up until young adulthood. That is, from around 5 to 12 years old. The children of this age who are mentioned in the Bible all had some kind of experience of God intervening in their everyday life.

For example, in John 6:9 we read that a young boy gives up his packed lunch for a crowd. He was there, watching as his small lunch was transformed into a meal large enough to feed 5,000 men and many more women and children.

In Mark 5, Jarius' daughter was raised from the dead and had an experience of God that would be remembered for many years to come. She experienced God's power working in her body to bring her back to life.

Every time Jesus taught and performed miracles, He didn't have an adult-only audience – there were children present too. When He needed a child as a visual aid, He didn't have to hire one from the local acting agency, there was one on hand ready to step in. People wanted their children to be around Jesus, even if the disciples considered children to be a nuisance amidst all that was going on.

Children were present wherever Jesus went, and they saw God at work. They heard Jesus' stories. They watched people responding to Him. Sometimes they were the recipients of miracles or deliverance. Other times they watched their aunty, uncle or friend-of-the-family be transformed.

This did not stop after Jesus went to heaven. As mentioned earlier, children may well have been in the upper room waiting for God to come and they were certainly among the crowd of 3,000 who responded to the Gospel on the day of Pentecost.

In Acts 16:25-34, the jailer's family felt the earthquake which led to the prison doors being thrown open. They met Paul and Silas who came out of the jail and into their home to preach the Gospel and they were among those who were baptized. Imagine the impact on their young children: first an earthquake wakes them, then the presence of God envelops them. This would be a day they would remember for the rest of their lives.

In the Old Testament we read of children who were experiencing God for themselves.

We read in 2 Kings 5:2–3 that Naaman came to Israel to seek the prophet who could heal him from his leprosy, but it was a young girl who suggested he should go. She watched her master grow sick with leprosy and knew that God could heal him. She saw him leave sick and return healed by the power of God. This experience would become a part of her faith journey; evidence of the reality of God stepping into everyday life.

Samuel heard God speaking to him when he was a young boy. This first prophecy was later fulfilled before his very eyes. This prophetic message was not simply a nice "spiritual moment" to write about in his journal, it was a faith-forming moment that pointed to the reality of God's intervention in the nation of Israel and the possibility of having a relationship with God in a time when visions were rare (1 Samuel 3:1).

As a shepherd boy David had seen God's deliverance in the fields on many occasions while tending his sheep. It was this confidence in the reality and goodness of God that led to him take on Goliath and ultimately become king.

Children in history

Throughout Church history children have encountered and experienced the reality of God at work. Some of the scenes are very dramatic, such as the children in the Scottish revivals who encountered God, or those of the Welsh revival who saw the dramatic change in their nation as people turned from crime and alcohol to praising and worshipping God.

One story from the Welsh revival records how the donkeys working the mines started to be treated so well by the miners that those whose job it was to take care of the donkeys feared for their jobs. The donkeys were used to being kicked and sworn at, but now were treated gently and kindly. The children would have witnessed a similar transformation in the adult's lives as God moved in that nation.

In the book *Visions beyond the Veil*, H. A. Baker records the remarkable stories of children in an orphanage in China who started to see open visions of heaven and hell.

In France, at the end of the 17th Century, a group of children were raised up who had prophetic visions of the troubles that were coming their way. Dubbed *les petits prophets* they would warn of soldiers coming to attack, giving time for Bibles to be hidden and families to escape before trouble arrived.

Around the same time in Sweden, 'the shouters' were a group of unschooled children who would shout out Bible verses they had never read to people passing by, encouraging them to repent and turn to God.

Today, God still wants to reveal Himself to our children. As they grow in the environment of the church there will be moments in their lives where they experience God's hand at work, or see God working in the life of someone they know. It may be a profound miracle, or it may be a simple answer to prayer. Either way, it is something that helps to form their faith in God.

This stage of faith development is important, because children need to know God is real. As they grow older they learn to tell the difference between something imaginary and something real: the Easter bunny is an imaginary character, but their school teacher is a real person. At this stage of life, they will have to make a decision about God. Will He end up in the make-believe box or the real box? Their spiritual experiences will be a key part of this.

One young boy came to a week-long camp. He had a very trouble background and initially wanted nothing to do with God. By the end of the camp, many children had experienced the presence of God in a tangible way. Some had been supernaturally healed, others had seen visions of God. But this boy's testimony was the most moving. He simply said: "I feel happier." These words encapsulated the transformation that had taken place in his life as he had experienced God for the first time.

Children today

We can create an environment where our children have the opportunity to experience God, as well as hearing about our ongoing experiences with Him. This may be as simple as recording the prayers we are praying, so that we are more aware when God has answered them.

When God answers our prayers as a family, or reveals Himself in a special way, we will need to keep a record of what our children have seen. We've already seen the importance of remembering what God has done. Like the Israelites in the desert, we are prone to focus on the problems in front of us and forget the times we have seen of God at work. These experiences can feed back into the memorial objects we have, where children are reminded of God's work in their lives. These stories become a part of their heritage, and even their children's heritage, as they grow with God.

Remember, the stories you have can be passed on to your children. As your children grow older, do they know when you chose to follow Christ? Are there any key testimonies from your life that you can share with them, that will encourage their faith? You never know – your children may be the ones to remind *you* of the testimonies when you need to hear them the most, or your story may be the very thing that encourages them as they form their own stories with God.

This second stage of faith formation, a personal experience of God, prepares them for stepping up into stage three as they reach young adulthood.

THOUGHTS TO PONDER

1. What experiences of God have you had?
2. What experiences of God have your children had?
3. Do you share these stories together to remind each other of what God has done?

Thank you, Lord, that you are at work today.

Thank you for the difference you have made to my life.

Help my children to experience you for themselves and see you at work in their lives.

"That which was from the beginning, which we have heard, which we have seen with our eyes, which we have looked upon, and our hands have handled, concerning the Word of life – the life was manifested, and we have seen, and bear witness, and declare to you that eternal life which was with the Father and was manifested to us – that which we have seen and heard we declare to you, that you also may have fellowship with us; and truly our fellowship is with the Father and with His Son Jesus Christ. And these things we write to you that your joy may be full."

(1 John 1:1–4)

13

SPIRITUAL ADVENTURE

Made to be radical

The third phase of faith development found in Scripture takes place as our children reach young adulthood. In Jewish culture this happens at the age of 13, for young men, and 12 for young women. At this stage, their faith needs to grow legs as they step out to have adventures with God.

The clearest example of this in Scripture is David and Goliath. While many children's picture Bibles depict David as a boy, it is more likely he was a young adult. Too young to fight as a soldier, but old enough to be sent on errands. King Saul was desperate, but not so desperate as to send a five-year-old into battle! So, while David had clearly not reached the peak of his physical fitness, he was not a young child. In all likelihood he was what we now term a teenager. His muscle mass had not yet built up and he was described as a youth by King Saul in 1 Samuel 17:33.

David chose to face a do-or-die moment in his life. He put himself in a situation where either God came through or he would be killed. Until this moment, David's experience of God's protection was all in response to the many dangers that had come to him. Wild animals had come onto his territory and God had strengthened and equipped David to face them. Now he was stepping out to face a challenge and initiating the attack. He would have been nervous, but he also had confidence in God. In future battles, we can imagine David looking back on this event as a faith-forming moment in his life. This is the moment when his faith grew legs and walked into danger.

In the same way we see Gideon stepping out in faith in Judges 6:25–27. The angel of the Lord appears to Gideon and instructs him to chop down the Asherah pole and destroy the altar to Baal at the end of his father's garden. Gideon is scared. He knows that if he does this and God doesn't back him up, he will be killed. Indeed, in verse 30 this is exactly what the men want to do with him. Yet Gideon steps out, trusting that God will turn up.

I picture him replying to the angel, "I will go... at night... with my friends." His faith is growing legs (that feel like jelly) for this daring expedition. He is scared, but he goes anyway.

Imagine if we were to give our young people this kind of opportunity to serve God. I am not saying that we seek to publicly humiliate our children (most teenagers feel their parents don't need to work too hard on that). Nor am I suggesting that we deliberately put them in harm's way, sending them into a warzone to see if their faith in God is strong enough to get them out alive! But we can create opportunities to encourage them out of their comfort zones and into dependence on God, where either He turns up or they look foolish.

This is not setting them up to fail, rather it is building on their past experiences, allowing their faith to grow legs. Whether it is travelling overseas to go on mission or delivering a word of knowledge to a stranger on the street, there are plenty of ways we can create opportunities for God-adventures.

This is the pattern of many of the young people in the Bible. Ruth set out on a journey with her mother-in-law which had an uncertain ending, but she was determined to make Naomi's God her God, and God took care of her.

Esther became queen at a young age (potentially around the age of 14) and five years later had to face her fear to save her people (and God took care of her).

Daniel and his friends were teenagers when they were taken into captivity. Here they chose to make a stand and refused to eat the choice food presented to them. This could have landed them in trouble, but instead God blessed them and took care of them.

You can read more stories of young people being used by God today in *The Josiah Generation*.

Young people love to be radical. They want to make a difference and generally have not yet been tempered by failure to slow them down. If we allow them, they can have opportunities to step out with God and this in turn will shape their faith.

Growing in faith

Imagine a young adult who has been through these three stages of faith formation as they have grown up. From when they were in the womb they have been exposed to the presence of God. As a child they have had clear experiences of God and, as a young adult, they have had adventures with God. Having experienced the reality of God in such a clear and personal way there is little room for doubting His existence or His ability to intervene.

Having experienced God's supernatural power at work in and through their lives, it would require a huge degree of mental gymnastics to explain away the hand of God. Their testimony can be the most powerful testimony any believer could have: "I have followed God faithfully for as long as I can remember." As Samuel put it in 1 Samuel 12:2: "I am old and gray headed, and look, my sons are with you. I have walked before you from my childhood to this day."

This is not to say that there won't be questions along the way, or even bumps on the road, but there will be clear signposts they can look back to, that point to God's continuing intervention in their lives. These experiences act as foundation stones for their faith in Jesus.

Jumping steps

It may be as you read this that you think of your children who are already growing up. Perhaps your child has already passed the age of spiritual exposure and spiritual experience without receiving either of these and is now supposed to be heading for a spiritual adventure, but has not been prepared for it. Is it possible to catch up on what your child has missed out on? Does your child have to go through these steps in the right order to benefit from them?

Clearly, these steps are not prerequisites to salvation, or guarantees of future faith. Each of our children, and each of our families, will have a different path to take. However, whatever age your children are, you can be intentional about exposing them to the presence of God, telling them of your experiences (and reminding them of theirs). As they grow older you can provide opportunities for them to have adventures with God.

In the Jewish way of life these things happen intentionally through the pattern of the feasts and as they transition to adulthood (bar/bat mitzvah). We will be considering this process of transition to adulthood in more detail in the subsequent chapters.

THOUGHTS TO PONDER

1. What opportunities have been the most important in your walk with God?
2. What opportunities could you provide for your teenagers to step out in faith?
3. What preparation would they need before this happens?
4. How can you help them to process their experiences for the future?

Lord, give my children the courage to face their fears,

The courage to stand up for you,

The courage to be true to themselves in every situation.

"He [Jesus] sent them [His disciples] to preach the kingdom of God and to heal the sick... So they departed and went through the towns, preaching the gospel and healing everywhere."

(Luke 9:2,6)

At home with God

14

TRANSITIONING TO ADULTHOOD

Teenagers are not biblical

Teenagers are not biblical. A study of the Bible will reveal that the word 'teenager' does not exist anywhere in any verse. Teenagers are a modern creation in a world where fulltime education continues into the twenties. These half-child, half-adult creatures tend to be nocturnal by nature. I recently heard one parent describe a teenager as a toddler in an adult body. Parents expect their children to act like adults, but treat them like children… sometimes. This kind of confusion does not help parents or their teenage children.

Jewish practice eliminates this confusion. As with many cultures around the world, the Jews have a clearly defined moment where you transition from childhood to adulthood. For the Jewish man this is known as the *bar mitzvah*, which literally means 'son of the commandment.' From this moment on they are responsible for their own actions.

The bar mitzvah is a huge celebration in Jewish families. It is not uncommon for a Jewish family to spend as much on a bar mitzvah celebration as one would spend on a wedding. The costs are so great that many Jews start saving for this as soon as their child is born.

Before the bar mitzvah a young person is a boy, and after the bar mitzvah he is a man. A Jewish son who has undergone his bar mitzvah can be one of the 10 men required to make up a quorum of people known as the *minyan*. This is required for public prayers and various other public expressions of faith. So, ten young men aged 13 could come together to make the minyan.

Women celebrate their *bat mitzvah* in a similar way, at the age of 12 or 13, depending on their traditions.

All this is in line with the Bible which repeatedly recognizes two age groups in society: children and adults. Adults are then subdivided into young adults and old adults, but they are still adults. In other words, a young adult is responsible for their actions, but is not alone in their decision making. Just because you have turned 13, this does not mean you will be kicked out of your home and expected to get a job. Rather, there is a need for mentoring as each person gets used to adulthood responsibilities and decision making.

Rituals of transition

In times past, young adults would become apprentices, but with the prolonging of further education, this no longer signals the coming of adulthood. It could be argued that when a woman begins menstruating this is a sign of adulthood, but this still leaves boys adrift. The only rituals a young man can point to in order to prove his manhood in Western culture is drunkenness and the loss of virginity. While I am not saying this is the only causes of such behavior, the desire to prove they are 'grown up' is certainly a factor.

Jewish culture recognizes different transitions in life:

- from womb to world
- childhood to adulthood
- singleness to marriage
- life to death on earth

Western culture has specific rituals for three of these transitions, but transitioning to adulthood does not have the same degree of clarity.

When a baby is born, a lot of community support is provided to help with the transition: the mother-in-law comes to stay. Midwives and health visitors are on hand to give advice and support groups are joined. Some churches have food rotas to provide weeks of food for the new family as they settle into a routine. The church offers dedication ceremonies and naming ceremonies.

When it comes to marriage the church provides pre-marriage counselling and helps celebrate the wedding day. Whole courses have been written to support the soon-to-be-married.

As death approaches, ministers are available for counsel. Most hospitals have chaplains available to provide spiritual care for this end of life period. Family and friends gather together to support the dying and their loved ones. Even a funeral service provides help with the transition to a new season for grieving relatives.

Yet, when it comes to the transition into adulthood, no one is quite sure exactly when it happens. Is it when they move out from home? Or when they get their first job? Or when they can legally vote? The transition phase lacks a ritual celebration and this leads to a prolonged phase of transition and, ultimately, confusion.

Celebrating adulthood

In our home we decided to develop a ritual for transition. As our children turn twelve years old we spend a year focusing on what it means to be an adult. We discuss how every freedom comes with responsibility. We look at how the kings of Judah and Israel carried their responsibilities: some ruled with selfish ambition, others ruled on behalf of their people. We also take time to discuss the way we treat the opposite sex, dating and sexual intercourse. All of this is in preparation for the upcoming ritual.

When our first son had his manhood ceremony, we decided that he should be affirmed as a man in the company of men. We wanted to do something that would be memorable in years to come and decided to hire a boat for the occasion. I invited some of my friends and people who had been influential in his life growing up, and asked each person to bring a Bible verse, a prophetic gift or a word of encouragement as Joshua entered into manhood.

One man brought a torch and a Swiss army knife. "God has given you His Word to guide you in life, and He has given you all the tools for everything that will come your way," he explained.

I gave Joshua a pen: "Up until this point your life has been written in pencil. Mistakes you make have been covered and erased by your parents. As you enter manhood there is a new permanence to your life. If you make a mistake, you will always be forgiven and accepted, but you will also have to live with the consequences of the mistakes you make," I told him. "But this is not all negative. When you do something good that affects the lives of others, that work will last into eternity."

We shared lots, ate lots, and laughed lots together, before praying for Joshua and blessing him as a young man. This ceremony had a lasting impact on his perception of himself and therefore on his responsibility and behavior. Having had the ceremony and declared Joshua a man, we now had to treat him like a man. In some ways, this challenge was more poignant. How could we as parents welcome him to adulthood? We will discuss this in the next chapter.

THOUGHTS TO PONDER

1. What negative stereotypes have you believed about the teenage season?
2. What kind of relationship would you like to have with your children when they are teenagers?
3. How can you help them to transition from childhood to adulthood?

Lord, I reject the world's stereotype for my children's teenager years.

May their teenage years be years of fruitfulness, not futility.

May they accept responsibility for their lives as adults and may they deepen their relationship with You.

"And the child Samuel grew in stature, and in favor both with the Lord and men."

(1 Samuel 2:26)

15

WELCOME TO ADULTHOOD

Practical changes

A ceremony is an important line in the sand; a defining moment that stands out from all the other days. For its impact to truly be felt, there should be a difference between the before and after. This is clear in all the other transitions of life that we have mentioned. Before you are born you are in the womb, after birth you are in the world. Before you are married you live apart, after you are married you live together. These changes emphasize the shift that took place in the ceremony.

Assuming that we are not going to evict our children at the age of 13, what kind of changes can we make to mark this difference? This is what we did with Joshua:

Firstly, we tried to find practical ways that would mark the transition in everyday life. We waited until this time before we gave him his own key to the house. He now had the freedom to come and go as he wished. This freedom was linked to the responsibility to tell us where he was going and to make wise choices.

We abolished bedtimes. I know, this is pretty radical, but we chose to let him decide when to go to bed. As I have shared this with various people, some have reacted in shock. You can hear them thinking, "This would not work in my house." But this freedom was conditional on him meeting his responsibilities. He had a responsibility to be up, dressed, alert, clean, prayed up and on time for school. If he was unable to meet this responsibility, he would lose the freedom that came with it.

When my second son reached thirteen we were obliged to drop his bedtimes too (if you parent more than one child, you will know the importance of being fair and keeping milestones the same for all your children). As a parent I was not sure if he was ready for this, but we had decided this was the age when it would happen and we had to stick to it. I didn't let on to my son what I was thinking, but I stood ready to reinstate bedtimes when he failed to wake on time. After all, this was the member of the family who was always last to rise; the one member who, since the age of eight, has had to be woken by us every morning to be ready on time.

On the night of his thirteenth birthday I reminded him that I would not be waking him up anymore – it was his responsibility to get up on time. As I went to bed I wondered if we were setting him up to fail and ourselves up for disaster. How wrong I was! The first morning, my son was up and ready to go fifteen minutes early. But would this last? That night he looked at the clock at 8:30pm and said, "I'm feeling tired tonight, I think I'll go to bed."

I was in shock. What had happened to my son? He still loves a lie-in when he doesn't have school the next day, but he was taking responsibility. As we reflected on this, we realized that we had blessed him into the stage of adulthood, telling him, "We believe in you son. You can do this." He had heard that message loud and clear and risen to the occasion.

This is a very adult concept. As an adult I have absolute freedom as to when I go to bed. If, however, I am unable to go to bed at a sensible time, so that I arrive at work persistently late or tired, I will not last in my job for long. Without a job I will lose the freedom and benefits that come from having income (namely food and shelter). The choice is mine, but if I take my responsibilities seriously I can enjoy my freedom liberally. A failure to meet my responsibilities leads to a loss of enjoyment of freedom.

As part of our ministry's discipleship of young men, we started a boys-to-men transition year. Among other things, this year we included a wilderness weekend, where we took the boys camping. This principle of freedom and responsibility was a big part of the weekend. Each tent was given the responsibility to wash up after each meal. We did not nag them, we simply told them whose turn it was and expected them to remember.

One group proudly did the washing up one evening, but couldn't be bothered to put the camping gear away. We didn't remind them what to do, they knew what was expected of them.

We just left everything out. The next morning, a delicious breakfast was cooking and everyone was hungry. Unfortunately, we had only supplied enough crockery for one meal and the bowls that had been left out overnight were now filled with water and insects. Those who had washed up the night before, started to complain that breakfast wasn't ready. "It is ready, we're just waiting for the bowls from last night's meal to be cleaned," one leader smiled.

"But we washed them last night!" one boy complained.

"Do you want to eat out of this?" the leader asked, highlighting the wildlife that was currently doing backstroke in the bowl. "You may have washed up, but you were also supposed to pack everything away. If you had finished the job this wouldn't have happened."

"We're not washing up again," they said.

"Then we won't be able to eat breakfast, and the longer you wait, those cooking the food will either have to take if off the fire so that it goes cold, or leave it so it burns. The choice is yours."

Looking at the glares of the rest of the group, it didn't take long before they rolled up their sleeves and got on with the job with minimal complaint. They were learning how their decisions affect others and were discovering the importance of managing their responsibilities.

Soft changes

Changes to bedtimes, having a house key and various other practical changes that we brought into our home, were one important aspect of acknowledging that this person in our house was now a *bona fide* adult. These practical changes were relatively easy to implement and were responded to well (especially as they all involved extra freedom in some way).

The harder changes to make were what I call the *soft changes*. This includes the way we speak to our children and help them to make decisions. Like many parents, we have always tried to encourage our children to make their own decisions. As toddlers they could decide, within reason, what they wanted to wear. As young children they could choose, within reason, birthday presents for their friends. As older children they could decide, within reason, what they spent their pocket money on. Each one could decide, within reason, on different activities we would do as a family. Now they had reached adulthood we wanted them to feel like they were completely in the driving seat of their lives.

How could we do this while still being involved of their lives?

Here we see the Bible pattern of young men and old men. Joel 2:28 speaks about the young men being the visionaries. They have vision and energy to fulfil their vision. "Let's end world hunger." The older men come with their wisdom and experience. They may dream, "Wouldn't it be great if one day there was no hunger in the world."

When the two meet it leads to a dynamic release for everyone. The older generation can encourage the younger ones, "That would be great, but let's start by ending hunger in our community." The younger generation can throw their youthful energy and enthusiasm into getting the job done.

How could we replicate this in our family? We realized that we would have to give our children the freedom to make mistakes, but that we still need to be on hand to listen, encourage, cheer them on and give them some wisdom. So, we can still sit with our son and say, "If you do this this way, it may end up with you being harmed, but if you do this instead, you may come out better." At the end of such discussions, we want him to understand that though we have laid out the potential consequences we can see (due to our experience), the decision will still fall to him.

The end product

Throughout this process we are constantly thinking, "What is the end product? What are we trying to achieve?" When we know where we are heading it informs the steps we take at the different stages of our children's lives. For example, when our children are first born we don't let them watch whatever they want to online, but by the time they leave home they will have the freedom to watch whatever they want, whenever they want. When that time comes, we want them to have the discernment to choose to watch things that are wholesome, not spiritually destructive. Giving them the tools they require to manage this responsibility wisely will happen gradually over time if we are intentional in preparing them for their future.

This early stage of adulthood is about preparing them for a time when they will live without us. When things don't work out as they expect, this is a learning opportunity. If they mess up (or should I say when they mess up), we want them to know that we still believe in them.

Remember, whatever season our children pass through, it is not a life sentence. The life sentence is the call of God on their lives. Early on in our parenting journey, we made a decision that we would not define our children by the negative aspects of their characters, but by their potential. As mentioned in Chapter Three, when they threw a huge tantrum in the middle of the supermarket as a toddler we didn't define their lives by those 20 minutes of embarrassing tantrum. Instead we chose to define them by the 23 hours and 40 minutes they'd had of being lovely.

We seek to do the same in the young adult season. They may be moody at times, but we will define them by those glimpses of the adult they are becoming. By declaring that our children have now become adults we are shouting to them, "We believe in you. We believe you have what it takes for this next season of life and we are here with you to support you on this journey."

Helping us to navigate this path, we draw on our experience working with other people's teenagers. We try to think how we would speak to someone else's child who we are mentoring. What would we pull them up on and what would we just let pass? This helps us to be involved whilst giving freedom.

Forming faith

As young adults, a key part of faith formation is found in the wider church community. Meeting not only with other young adults, but people of all ages who love Jesus, is a key part of growing in God. We have always desired for our children to have role models outside of our family, who are one step ahead of them in age and their pursuit of God. When they were aged around ten, we wanted them to have godly thirteen-year-olds to look up to. When they are fifteen we want them to mix with those turning twenty. All this helps give them a vision of what life might be like for them in that phase of life, as well as having someone to relate to who is closer to their current season of life.

One of our children was helping with the children's work and many of the children in the group were looking up to him with admiration. We pointed out to him that he did exactly the same when he was their age, reminding him of godly young adults he had known when he was a child. It was great to see the smile on his face as he remembered the impact other young people had on him when he was a small child. He saw that he could have an impact on these children, as others had on him.

Sometimes as parents we can wonder what our role is in faith development at this stage of our children's lives. Yet, when we follow the Jewish model of passing on faith, it works well in this season of life too. The daily, weekly and annual rhythms provide a framework for family life. The memorial objects will still exist in our home and the feasts will still be celebrated. Our role as warriors, interceding on their behalf, will continue for as long as we are still on earth. The joy of finding environments where they can adventure with God is still our privilege as we mentor our children. The power of blessing our teenagers still speaks into and affects their lives.

I was blessed when I travelled to Sicily to meet a wonderful, godly family. The Italians love to greet each other with a kiss and when this couple's three children turned up, the two younger children were quick to greet their parents. Their oldest son, who was around seventeen at the time, was more reluctant. His mother called him over and requested her greeting. You could tell that he clearly hated it, yet secretly loved it. He didn't want to initiate it, but it stopped him from being isolated and reminded him that he was loved. This may not be a part of our culture, but we can make it a part of our culture to bless our children each week and hug them regularly.

Am I too late?

As you've been reading through this section you may be wondering if it is too late to begin. As one parent said, "My child is fifteen and we have never done an adult ceremony – have we missed it?"

I want to encourage you to have one, regardless of how old they are. It is never too late to affirm our children as adults and to encourage them.

THOUGHTS TO PONDER

1. What changes could you make to your parenting in the teenage years?
2. What are you doing now to prepare your children for a time when they no longer live at home with you?
3. What are the most important qualities for you to instill in your children for their future?

Lord, you have blessed me with my children for a season, but they are yours for a lifetime.

Help me to prepare them for their future.

Give me wisdom with each new challenge that comes.

"My son, hear the instruction of your father, and do not forsake the law of your mother; for they will be a graceful ornament on your head, and chains about your neck."

(Proverbs 1:8–9)

Welcome to adulthood

At home with God

PART 4
THE FAMILY IN CONTEXT

16

YOU MATTER

Pause points

Family is such an important part of God's plan for raising up the generations, but it can also be a place of great tension. Strong families do not become strong by accident, they are intentional in the way that they work together.

The founding part of many Christian families is the marriage covenant. If you are the sole parent raising your children, you may want to skip straight to the next section.

If there are two of you, then there are a number of pitfalls that can occur within marriage. Our children very quickly work out which parent to ask for what. "If I need money, I have to ask Dad. If I want to go on the computer, I have to ask Mum." It is very easy for children to come between the marriage relationship. Yet this does not help the child to grow into a rounded person. If one parent says "no," then the other parent should support this, at least in front of the children. It may lead to a private discussion to re-evaluate the boundaries you can both agree on and stick to.

Marriage is a covenant, which means team-work; working together to support each other. Of course, that's the ideal. It doesn't always work out that way. It may be that you are no longer able to negotiate boundaries with your spouse, but when you make time to invest in your marriage by spending time together, it can make the harder conversations easier.

When you take time out together, away from the children, and come back stronger together, your children benefit. Whether this is an annual weekend away or a weekly date night, investing in your marriage is good for your sanity and for your children's welfare.

My wife and I were surprised when our children reached their teenage years. As young children we tucked them into bed by 7pm and enjoyed the whole evening alone together. However, the older they get, the later they stay up. We realized we had lost our precious evenings and instituted a Mum and Dad only evening.

By creating these pause points in family life, where husband and wife can be together, you are sowing not just into your marriage, but indirectly into your children's lives.

Paul gives the balance of how much responsibility rests with us, when it comes to living with others. He makes it clear that it is our role to live at peace with everybody, but at the same time he acknowledges that this is not always the reality. Romans 8:12 says, "If it is possible, *as much as depends on you*, live peaceably with all men."

Where there are tensions, we are responsible before God to do all we can to keep the peace. Having done this, we are not to carry any guilt for a lack of peace. The prayer, "Lord change me," is a far more powerful prayer in most marriages than "Lord, change them."

One person joked, "A woman marries a man believing she can change him, but soon finds out she can't. A man marries a woman, hoping she will never change, but soon discovers that she does." We do not have control over our spouse or their actions, but we most certainly do have control over how *we* react and respond. Within a marriage, increasing godliness in one partner often spurs an increased godliness in the other.

I love the way Psalm 128:3 describes the difference between our relationship with our spouse and our children. "Your wife shall be like a fruitful vine in the very heart of your house, your children like olive plants all around your table."

As our children grown and flourish around our table they are like olive plants. We should enjoy the immediate fruits that they bear: that first step, the silly joke they made, the unique fashion sense they have chosen. Olives fresh from a tree can be enjoyed within a week (once they have been cured in brine).

Wives, however, are described as fruitful vines. A vine tree bears a lot of grapes. These grapes can be enjoyed immediately, but they can also be turned into wine, which gets better with age.

God's intention is that marriage gets better with age! This should be our vision and desire for our marriage and, as we invest in it together, we can both delight in this.

If we can recognize the different strengths each person brings into the family and celebrate those strengths, then our marriages will be strong and our children will benefit.

Jewish teachers speak often about the differences between men and women's roles. For example, Rabbi Lazer Gurkow from London, Ontario, says:

> *"Mothers and fathers parent in different ways. Mothers provide the nurturing love that builds confidence and enables personalities to flourish. Fathers provide the mentoring that directs our path and shows us right from wrong.*
>
> *(Of course, the mother and father roles are not exclusive – these are the typical features of each, but both fathers and mothers need to incorporate the other's style too, and often do)."*

The Jewish mama is known to be tough but caring. She gives out hugs continually, teaches her children, and knows it all in the home. As my Jewish grandmother used to say to my dad: *"Chicken soup is good for you. It won't kill you, but will make you better. After all, I made it!"* The Jewish mother is the glue of the Jewish family and therefore of the Jewish community.

One parent wonders

If you have felt judged by the church because you are parenting on your own, I am sorry that you have been hurt in this way. At times you have probably found an inner strength you didn't know you had, and at other times been pushed to extremes of emotion so that you don't know how you will cope. But the challenges you face are not insurmountable. You are not a second class or second-rate parent. Rather, you have unique promises from God that you can draw on.

For example, in Psalm 68:5 God promises to be a father to the fatherless. One mum I knew decided to take this promise into her family. Her teenage son had learnt that God was his father from when he was very young. He had seen Daddy God provide for him and take care of him.

One afternoon he was playing loud music in the house. His mum did not approve of the music, or the volume at which it was being played. They got into an argument which only ended when the mum yelled at her son in exasperation, "Ask your Father!"

The young man sloped off to his room to pray. He came back an hour later and said, "Daddy God says I have to stop listening to the music for one month and then I can go back to listening again."

As a parent you matter. With so much of your life devoted to your children, I want to encourage you to take time for yourself. Build into your week adult company and me-time and don't allow yourself to feel guilty about bringing in a babysitter. Give yourself permission to have some time out as a parent. The housework will still be there tomorrow, but energy conserved today will prepare you to face the future together with your children.

Do lean on your wider family of church to help and support you. The community you are part of is an important part of God's planned support for you. We discuss this further in the next chapter.

THOUGHTS TO PONDER

1. Do you take time out for yourself?
2. How are you investing in the adult relationships you have?

Lord, you know me and you know my situation.

Thank you that you made us to have friendships and companions.

Bless every member of my home and let peace reign in my house.

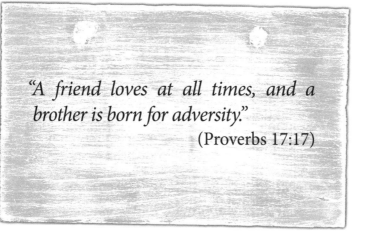

"A friend loves at all times, and a brother is born for adversity."
(Proverbs 17:17)

17

YOUR COMMUNITY MATTERS

What is family?

Back in Chapter One we saw that family was God's idea. The nuclear family, made up of parents and children, is the first separate unit that God created. That's why a man *leaves* his father and mother and is joined to his wife: they form a new family unit. This new unit is separate and distinct from the units these people have left, and is a unit that their children will join.

I used to picture society as a building made out of individual bricks, where each brick represents a person. However, as I saw how families are the base unit of God's society, I realized that this analogy is wrong. Each brick represents a single family, not an individual. When our families are broken, we are not simply rearranging individual bricks to sit apart from each other, the bricks themselves are being broken. This is why God seeks to restore families, places individuals in families, and instructs His people to take special care of those whose families are broken: the widows and orphans.

The Old Testament uses two main words to describe family. The first is *bayith*, which appears 2005 times. This word describes the family living under the same roof together. This definition readily extends beyond what we now term the nuclear family to include grandparents and servants. The Greek word, *oikos*, in the New Testament has a similar meaning. Appearing 114 times, it is often translated "household".

So far in this book, we have been considering this aspect of our families. This nuclear family is at the very center of child development. However, God does not intend families to be isolated units – He wants them to be set in the wider context of community.

The Hebrew word, *mishapchah*, refers to this. With 301 appearances it refers to the circle of people around a family household; people with whom heart and values are shared, support is found and life is lived. This wider community plays a key part in the passing on of faith.

Church is often described as the family of God, but this is more than a nice idea, this is what we are supposed to be: *family*. One leadership team that Helen and I were leading was going through a very challenging time. The team was made up of people who were as diverse as you can imagine: young and old, male and female, and with a full range of professions, educational achievements and ethnic backgrounds. There were very few common interests, other than our love for the Lord. Over a period of months, the tension in the group built as everyone tried to love each other, find their place and unite.

In one meeting the issue was blown wide open as one lady spoke out, "No one in this group is my friend." The lady continued, "If I want to hang out or have a coffee, I wouldn't choose anyone here. I have friends and that's who I want to spend time with. Frankly, I don't want or need friends from within this group."

At that moment my heart sunk. It felt like we had reached the lowest of the low. It seemed like our attempts to form friendships between us was finally being aborted. But the lady had not finished talking.

"I don't see anyone in this group as my friend. But if I was in trouble, I wouldn't go to my friends, I would come to you first: *you are my family.*"

She had hit the nail on the head and with that one sentence months of tension dissolved. We had been trying hard to be friends (and within the group some natural friendships were of course forming). We were not all going to get on in that way, but we were, and still are, family!

Within church we need each other.

Crossing generations

Earlier in the book we looked at the importance and power of intergenerational relationships. I made the comment that the most natural place for these relationships to flourish is in the family. This is the Jewish model of faith development. Yet this is not the only place where the generations mix. Our church communities provide the perfect place for the wider family to love and grow together. An elderly gentleman can receive a great sense of love and belonging when a young child is pleased to see him. The child in turn benefits from another grandparent figure in their life. Once they know each other's names, they may both have also found an intercessor who is faithful to them. These kinds of relationships can become a highlight of our children's church experience if we intentionally foster them.

You have probably already worked out that modern Jews love to feast together, just as Jesus did. Eating together is such a key part of many cultures. As a family we try to invite other people to join our family for meals. When we eat together and share together we also end up growing together. I love going to church after we have had a church member round at our house and watching the change in relationship that has taken place between them and my children. The warm greeting, the shared love and the looks of joy are all part of building the community of church.

Intentionally seeking to create these opportunities to love leads to greater love and understanding. This is one of the things that is supposed to mark out the church. Jesus put it this way in John 13:35: "By this all will know that you are My disciples, if you have love for one another."

To become a family that is outward looking is part of us taking our place in our church community. As we do this, we will definitely benefit ourselves.

I want to be like you

As I wrote earlier, one of the benefits I want for my children is for them to have people they look up to. Specifically, I want them to have people who are close to their age and moving into the next season of life. As toddlers, I want them to know children who are at school. When they are in primary school, I want them to know some teenagers. As teenagers, I want them to be friends with people who are at university. For myself, I want to relate to people who are retired.

Why? Because in doing so we have a model of how we can follow God in the next stage of our lives. We see some of the challenges we may face and some of the godly attitudes we need to develop in preparation for those times.

While my teenage children may value my wisdom and the experience that comes from the (many) years of life I have lived, they will appreciate someone who really gets their stage of life, because they have only just lived it themselves.

This is a godly model. The rabbi seeks disciples who can discover his way of thinking and follow his way of life, to leave a legacy. The apostle Paul put it this way: "Imitate me, just as I also imitate Christ" (1 Corinthians 11:1). Seeing a life lived for God, provides a real-life example of how life can be done. Reading the Bible might give you the theory, but watching someone who is living the Bible helps you to understand the practical application.

This is often a natural thing for us to do as parents. Many parents seek out other parents whose children are slightly older than their own and who seem to be "doing it right", so they can glean wisdom from them.

What a privilege it is if we can identify those who are living passionately for God, who are slightly older than our own children, and allow them to rub shoulders together. We have found these relationships to be very fruitful in the lives of our own children.

I know one family who intentionally adopt a university student. The student often ends up eating more meals with the family than in their own home. As the student navigates life away from home for the first time, the parents become like surrogate parents. Meanwhile, the student becomes like an older brother or sister to the children.

One teenager would frequently come to our house. Our children loved him and would happily jump on him as soon as he walked through the door. He often turned up following the trends of the day: his trousers would be half way down his waist and his underpants visible. We soon figured out that our children were looking up to him and aspiring to be like him.

"All teenagers wear their trousers like this," our six-year-old declared, wriggling his own trousers lower down his waist.

"No, they don't," we quickly replied.

This led to a great conversation with our friend. "You know our children really look up to you. They want to be like you and see you like an older brother."

The young lad was shocked and proud at the same time. We discussed how he was a good example to them in many ways, but in this one area his example was not so great. You could see he felt so honored by the fact that our children wanted to follow his example.

From then on, our doorstep greeting went something like this:

"Great to see you, pull up your trousers and come on in!"

He would laugh, pull up his trousers and come in. I'm pleased to say this young man has now grown up and his fashion sense has changed (for the better in my opinion). Even though we moved away almost a decade ago, he is still thought of very fondly by our children.

I am not alone

Another aspect of the wider community is that we can meet other people of a similar age to us who share our faith. Friendship is a key part of growing up. For many children, church friends are an important part of their faith development. They can let them know that they are not the only one their age following Christ.

During our years of working with children and young people, I have always been amazed at the quality of the friendships that are formed in church. When young people become passionate for God, their church friends become their best friends. They meet their church friends for a few hours a week and for the odd residential trip during the year. They see their school friends for six hours a day, every weekday in term time. Yet in spite of this, they become better friends with people who they spend less time with.

When God is at the center of our social lives, we draw closer to those who we spend time with. As parents we can encourage these godly relationships in very simple ways. Here are three simple ideas that will make a real difference to the friendships our children form within the church community.

1. Show up as regularly as you can for church meetings.
2. Let your children be part of every activity your church community runs for them.
3. Invite families around for Sunday lunch, so the children can have more time to play together.

Soaking up the atmosphere

When we stand outside on a snowy day, it gets harder to stay warm over time, even with many layers of clothing. Similarly, when we are in a warm room, it is hard to keep our coats on and remain comfortable.

The communities we are a part of will inevitably have an effect on our children's spiritual formation. If you are part of a community where people are passionately living out their faith, this is contagious. If you are part of a community where people only attend out of a religious duty, then like a cold day, this attitude can gradually permeate your family too.

Assuming that your community is not the one perfect church that exists in the world, what can we do to help our children get the most out of the church community?

Firstly, every church community has its strengths and weaknesses. As humans we are prone to dwell on the weaknesses while ignoring the strengths. If we flip this in our mind, and focus on the strengths, then we can start to appreciate them once more. As we appreciate these aspects of the church, it will come out in the way we talk about the church. This, in turn, will allow our children to acknowledge these things more quickly and allow them to rub off on them.

Secondly, find where the life is. In my experience, nearly every church community has at least a few people who are alive to God and hungry for more of Him. Whether they are the young minister who has just started out, or the ninety-year-old saint who prays daily for the church, these people are gems who are worth being with. Find those people and become their best friend. They will appreciate the encouragement from you and your family, as much as you appreciate theirs.

Pray for your leadership. Praying for church leadership is actually a selfish prayer: as the church leadership grow closer to

God and make more godly decisions, God pours out more of His Spirit on the church and every church member benefits. If you love your leaders, pray for them. If you disagree with them, pray for them (you may discover that their unique view of the church allows their decisions to be more right than you first thought).

Taking their place

Raising children in a society that generally rejects the worldview and values of Christianity can be challenging. We are not the first generation to face these issues, however, and God does not expect us to do this alone. He has given us the Holy Spirit and the rest of His family to help us. While it may not be perfect, and you may not see everyone in your church as your friend, they are your family.

In the words of Hebrews 10:24–25, "And let us consider one another in order to stir up love and good works, not forsaking the assembling of ourselves together, as is the manner of some, but exhorting one another, and so much the more as you see the Day approaching."

We should be intentional in seeking out relationships that will benefit our children. Grandparent figures who can provide stability; those who are slightly older than them who can provide an example; those who are their age, who can provide friendship; those who are younger than them, who they can model faith to. Church community may sometimes feel like hard work, but it is a valuable part of the faith development of every member of the family.

If you want to think about how to do this practically, re-read the section on co-ministers in Chapter Nine.

THOUGHTS TO PONDER

1. Which parents in your church community can you learn from and seek advice from?
2. Who do your children look up to?
3. What are the strengths of your church community?

Lord, thank you for the community you have placed around me.

Thank you for supportive friends and wise leaders.

Help my family to be open and welcoming to other members of the church community.

"For as the body is one and has many members, but all the members of that one body, being many, are one body, so also is Christ."

(1 Corinthians 12:12)

18

AND FINALLY...

Enjoy the journey

Parenting is meant to be fun. We all know that it can be exhausting and at times infuriating, but it is also meant to be joyful. The typical Jewish home will often be full of laughter, stories, and more laughter. A huge part of Jewish culture is their humor. After all, Proverbs 17:22 tells us that, "A merry heart does good, like medicine."

Humor sets and reinforces culture. It pulls on stereotypes and builds identity. An American Jewish identity survey[1] in 2013 found that 42 percent of American Jews consider "having a good sense of humor" to be "an essential part of what being Jewish means." (In contrast, only 19 percent said observing Jewish law was essential.) In the appendices of this book you can get a taste of Jewish humor for yourself.

Finding the joy on the journey is important. You are a parent and it is hard work, so you may as well enjoy it at the same time. Why not try to remember those funny moments for the times when you need it most?

It was 2 o'clock in the morning when Helen and I woke to the sound of crashing glass. Living in an area where thieves had been breaking into homes, Helen bravely nudged me out of bed and encouraged me to go downstairs while she stayed upstairs, ready to call the police if I needed backup. As I entered the kitchen, nothing could have prepared me for what I was about to face.

Peering through a plume of white smoke I saw in the middle of the floor broken eggs, a huge pile of sugar and several empty bags of flour (the cause of the "smoke"). The jagged edges of a glass coco jar sat to one side, where coco had been spilled, and in the middle of it all was my two-year-old son.

"What are you doing?" I yelled.

---

[1] http://www.pewforum.org/files/2013/10/jewish-american-survey-full-report.pdf

Through the flour cloud, the ghost-like toddler looked at me with large innocent eyes.

"I'm making a cake for you, Daddy."

At that moment my heart melted and I could not be angry. Carefully lifting him up to avoid the broken glass, I gave him a big cuddle. (Secretly, I was impressed that he had gathered so many of the right ingredients for a cake – his observational cookery lessons with Mummy were clearly paying off.)

What's the point of telling you this story? It reinforces one of our values of looking out for each other. It's fun and it's a part of our heritage as a family.

As is the time one of our toddlers came downstairs naked and covered in chocolate he had managed to sneak away into a secret stash.

"Have you been eating chocolate?" we asked, suppressing our grins.

"No!" an innocent voice protested.

When just over a decade later we discovered the same child had hidden chocolates from the Christmas box in his room, we couldn't help but reminisce about how nothing much had changed.

"But Dad," he protested in his deep voice, "at least this time I came down wearing clothes!"

For that, we were all incredibly grateful.

Bringing joy to the family can help diffuse conflict. Our son Simeon is a skilled comedian, timing his jokes to perfection. He has used humor many times to his advantage: it's hard to tell someone off while you are crying with laughter.

Find joy in the moment and savor those times that remind you what a privilege it is to be a parent. Children are a gift from the Lord. The fruit of the womb is His reward. God has blessed you with your bundles of joy. Enjoy them as they grow.

God believes in you

Remember where we began. Family is God's idea and God believes in you. He believes that you have what it takes to help your children become who He has called them to be. He did not make a mistake when He gave you your particular mix of children, nor did He overestimate your ability to nurture them. You may feel like you are struggling at times, but God believes in you!

Nobody is better positioned to raise your children than you and you can do this. Earlier in this book I spoke about our children being like arrows, aimed for a target. When you are releasing an arrow from the bow, one degree of change in the aim can make a huge difference to the end result.

Remember also that every family is different. Though the principles in this book are found in many Jewish homes, the outworking of the principles are different in every single family. Give a set of tools and some wood to three different craftsmen and you will end up with three very different products as each of them exerts their unique skillset, experience and personal preferences.

The framework for faith development that God has provided works with every type of personality and family. Using these same tools in your own unique way will create the next generation of spiritual giants.

This book is packed full of information and ideas for different stages of the parenting journey. In the first appendix you will find a checklist of many of these ideas. As you come to the end of the book, reflect on what small changes you can make to your family life. They may seem tiny in implementation, but over time such changes can have a giant effect on the future.

Why not decide to reassess your parenting every six months? Make a note in your diary for six months from now to see how you have got on and consider what else you can introduce or tighten up on. The checklist in the appendix can act as a shortcut for you to revisit the ideas and concepts in this book without having to re-read the whole thing (to read this once is enough of an achievement for most busy parents!)

When Helen and I noticed that we were having to encourage our children to say please and thank you an average of 100 times a day, we reflected on why. We soon realized that we were not modelling it to them. Once we changed our behavior, they soon copied us.

When our children were shouting at us and discipline involved an ever-increasing escalation of voices, we decided to make a small change and buck the trend. The louder the children got, the more softly spoken we became. It didn't take long for the cycle to be broken.

"Dad, I don't like it when you speak to me in that quiet tone," one son said to me through gritted teeth.

"Why not?" I asked, curious as to his observations on this small change we had recently made.

"Because when you speak quietly, I can't shout back."

I smiled to myself.

We are all on a journey, learning more about God and each other. We are not just here to help our children; our children will help us on our journey. Someone quipped that when you have children you develop levels of patience and self-control you would never need if you didn't have children!

Dedicated to God

As we intentionally structure our families to put God at the very center, and seek to raise our children in an environment where they are exposed to the presence of God on a regular basis, we will see our children grow into their God-given potential.

Proverbs 22:6 says, "Train up a child in the way he should go, and when he is old he will not depart from it." The Hebrew word translated 'train' is *hanak*. This word appears four other times in the Old Testament. In every place, except in this verse, it is translated as 'dedicate' and is used in the context of dedicating the temple or other items to the Lord.

The process of dedication involved sacrifice and setting aside specific time for the dedication. Three distinct steps were required: firstly, an object had to be placed in the temple, or sacrifices had to be made in the building. Secondly, prayers of dedication had to be made. Finally, the item had to remain there. If it was invaded, damaged or spoilt, then rededication would be required. In the light of this, some Jews would argue that *hanak* in this context involves nurturing as well as dedicating our children.

What if we were to pursue this same process for each of our children?

Firstly, we could bring them into the temple. By this, I don't mean the church building - I am sure your minister would not be happy if you turned up with all your children intending to leave them there. Rather, it is an environment where God is honored and His presence is welcomed. In other words, we are to bring our children into the presence of God.

Secondly, we should pray over our children, dedicating them to the Lord and to His work. This prayer is not so much a simple ceremony carried out before the church, as it is an ongoing process of covering our children in prayer.

Finally, it is important that we leave them in God's presence. If an event in school pulls them from God, or if they are damaged by the words of a friend, then we will have to rededicate them to the Lord, bringing them back into His presence.

In this context of continual, active, discipleship, Proverbs says that as we dedicate our children in God's ways, when they are old they will not depart from them.

May your children grow into their full potential in God and may they live to serve Him all the days of their lives. May you be blessed with joy in your family.

As the Jews would bless each other using the words of Numbers 6:24–26, I pray this prayer of blessing over you and your whole family:

> *The Lord bless you and keep you;*
> *The Lord make His face shine upon you,*
> *And be gracious to you;*
> *The Lord lift up His countenance upon you,*
> *And give you peace.*
> *Amen.*

THOUGHTS TO PONDER

1. What aspect of this book has impacted you the most?
2. What are you already doing that matches the principles in this book?
3. What small changed are you planning to make to your family as you disciple your children?

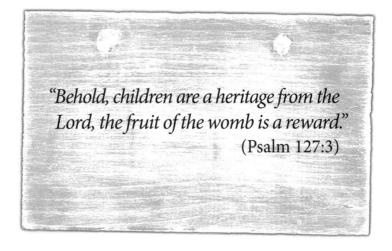

"Behold, children are a heritage from the Lord, the fruit of the womb is a reward."
(Psalm 127:3)

At home with God

PART 5

APPENDICES

CHECKLIST SUMMARY

This book is packed with concepts and ideas that you can use. We encourage you to take time to reflect on your parenting every six months or so. At this time, you may want to read through this list and decide which aspects you would like to introduce or make a focus for the next six months.

The numbers in brackets at the end of each principle tells you the chapter(s) where this issue was discussed, so you can flick back and read the relevant sections.

Having read through the book you may not be sure where to start. If you are currently doing nothing, I would encourage you to begin with these two areas:

- [ ] Pray for your children
  - [ ] Develop a daily rhythm of daily prayer (2, 10)
  - [ ] Remember the promises God has spoken over your children (10)
  - [ ] Bless your children (3)
  - [ ] Pray for them at times of transition (3)

- [ ] Hold a weekly family meal (Sabbath meal) (2)
  - [ ] Fun, food and faith (6)
  - [ ] Reading the Bible together (meat not just milk) (4, 7)
  - [ ] Prayers of blessing (3)
  - [ ] Space for them to hear from God (8)

Here are other areas that you may want to consider implementing or developing in your own way in your family.

☐ Let your children mix with other generations in a way that is safe and age appropriate (1)

☐ Talk about God in everyday life (4)
 ☐ Share your testimonies with your children (5)
 ☐ Share your family's spiritual history (5)
 ☐ Disciple your children when issues arise (4)
 ☐ Build heart connections with your children (2, 15)

☐ Put up memorial objects around your home (5)
 ☐ Records of answered payer (5)
 ☐ Key Bible verses (5)

☐ Celebrate the feasts (6)

☐ Encourage your children to have a time of daily devotion (8)

☐ Minister with your children and allow them to grow in areas of ministry in the church (9)

☐ Babies (11)
 ☐ Fill your home with worship
 ☐ Expose your babies to the presence of God

☐ Children (12)
 ☐ Let them experience the reality of God
 ☐ Record these moments to remind them in the future

☐ Teenagers (13)
 ☐ Release them to go on adventures and take time to debrief afterwards (13)
 ☐ Prepare for transition to adulthood (14)

☐ Hold a transition ceremony (14)

☐ Allow your parenting style to mature with them (15)

☐ Determine to look for the godliness in them (15)

☐ Make time for yourself, your spouse and other adult relationships (16)

☐ Be an active member of your local church community (17)

☐ Build relationships with people close to your children's age who love God and your children look up to (17)

☐ Talk with a family whose children are older than yours who you respect (17)

JEWISH HUMOR

The troubled father

A Jewish father was very troubled by the way his son turned out and went to see his rabbi about it.

"Rabbi, I brought him up in the faith, gave him a very expensive bar mitzvah and it cost me a fortune to educate him. Then he tells me last week, he's decided to be a Christian. Rabbi, what should I do?"

The rabbi strokes his beard and says, "Funny you should come to me. I too, brought up my son as a boy of faith, sent him to university and it cost me a fortune, then one day he comes to me and tells me he wants to be a Christian."

"What shall we do?" the man asked the rabbi.

"Let us go and see the Chief Rabbi," the Rabbi replied.

"Chief Rabbi, we brought our sons up in the faith, gave them very expensive bar mitzvahs and it cost us a fortune to educate them. Last week they told us they've decided to become Christians. Chief Rabbi, what should we do?"

The Chief Rabbi strokes his beard and says, "Funny you should come to me. I too, brought up my son as a boy of faith, sent him to university and it cost me a fortune, then one day he comes to me and tells me he wants to be a Christian."

"What should we do?" the rabbis ask.

"We will have to ask the Almighty."

"Jehovah, we brought our sons up in the faith, gave them a very expensive bar mitzvah and it cost us a fortune to educate them. Last week they told us they've decided to be Christians. Lord Almighty, what should we do?"

God replied, "Funny you should come to me..."

Human?

Q: In the Jewish doctrine, when does a fetus become a human?

A: When it graduates from medical school.

Breaking the rules

On the holiest day of the year, Yom Kippur, during the afternoon break between prayers, a Jew walking home from the synagogue passes by the golf course. He is overtaken by an urge to play some golf, and he says to himself, I'll play just one hole and I'm back to the synagogue. Amazingly, for the first time in his life he hits a hole-in-one.

The angels cry out to God: "What is happening here? A Jew desecrates the holiest day, and you reward him with a hole-in-one?!"

God answers: "True, but who's he going to tell?"

The priest and the rabbi

A Priest and a Rabbi are walking and admiring the scenery. The Rabbi asks the Priest what are his hopes and fantasy in life?

Priest: "Maybe to be a Bishop one day."

Rabbi: "And then?"

Priest: "Maybe even a Cardinal."

Rabbi: "And then?"

Priest: "Well, if am really, really lucky, the Pope himself."

Rabbi: "And then?"

Priest: (Starting to get really angry) "What else can I do? I can't become God!"

Rabbi: "Well, one of our boys did that."

The budget Bar Mitzvah

The father of a boy who is preparing for his Bar Mitzvah has a discussion with the synagogue rabbi about the ceremony.

The rabbi tells him how he will proceed: he will give a speech about the grandparents and parents of the boy, what *tzadikim* (just) and great people they are, and how much *tzdaka* they do for the community and how great the kid is the *hatan bar mitzvah*.

But, the rabbi says it won't be for free.

"How much would it cost?" asks the father.

"$2,000," says the rabbi.

"What? $2,000? You know how much I have to pay for the kosher catering, the party at night, the cameraman?" exclaims the father.

"Well," says the rabbi "I can make it much shorter. I wouldn't talk about the grandparents, only about you, your wife, and your son, and what great people you are, and I will only charge $1,000."

"$1,000?" exclaims the father, "we aren't rich people. Do you know how much the new outfit alone cost us? What can you do for $500?"

The rabbi thinks for a while then says:

"I can give a speech for $500, but then I will tell only the truth."

Converted

Two Jews walk in front of a church that has a sign "Convert today and receive $100".

One of them mocks the church for trying to lure new believers with money, but his friend says, "Why not? $100 is $100," and goes in.

After a while he comes out and his friend ask him, "So, did you receive the $100?"

The new Christian responds: "You Jews only ever think about the money!"

The Bar Mitzvah speech

Before I begin, I want you all to know that dad has instructed me not to be witty, not to be humorous, and not to be intellectual. In fact, he said, "Just be yourself."

Did they notice?

Lionel is getting quite bald and his daughter Sharon's bat mitzvah is coming up. All his friends and family will be there and even men can be vain, so he gets fitted with an expensive wig.

During the bat mitzvah party everything goes well. Nevertheless, Lionel thinks that everyone must have seen his wig. The next day, Sharon sees his worried look and asks, "What's the matter, Daddy? Why are you so sad?"

"I'm not really sad," he replies, "it's just that I'm sure yesterday everyone saw that I was wearing a wig."

"No, they didn't, Daddy," Sharon says. "No one I told knew."

Thirteen

One day, Moshe is walking past the wooden fence at the side of the local Mental Care Home for Jewish People, when he hears the residents inside chanting, "Thirteen! Thirteen! Thirteen!"

Moshe is quite a curious kind of man and wonders, "Is there a bar mitzvah going on inside?" so he searches for a suitable hole in the fence and then looks in. Immediately, someone on the other side of the fence pokes him in the eye with their finger.

Then the chanting begins again, "Fourteen! Fourteen! Fourteen!"

You're next

When Louis was younger, he just hated going to bar mitzvahs. All of his uncles and aunts would come up to him, poke him in the ribs, giggle, and say to him, "You're next, Louis."

They stopped doing that after Louis started doing the same thing to them at funerals.

How old are they?

A Jewish mother is walking her children in the park. "What cuties! How old are they?" asks a Jewish bubby.

"The rabbi is three, the doctor is five," she answers.

Give Me 5

Give Me 5 is bursting full of ideas that you can be used in children's church, youth church and family devotions. Written over a period of ten years, each activity has been tried and tested at local church level. It is packed full of activity ideas that you can use to creatively teach and develop children and young people in five different areas:

- Welcome
- Worship
- Word
- Warfare
- Witness.

This resource will help you and your family to engage creatively as you share about God together at home week by week.

The Josiah Generation

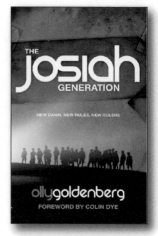

This book outlines a growing revolution in children's ministry, where children are not seen merely as the potential leaders of the Church of tomorrow, but as a vital, relevant part of the Church's ministry now. Examining the life of Josiah – who became king of Judah while still a boy – and using real life testimonies, this book will help prepare the Church to expect great things from this rising generation.

"Loved this book. It is well written and easy to read. I read it as a parent and found myself challenged to ensure I am stepping aside and doing all I can to encourage my children to have their own relationship with God; along with giving them the confidence to listen for His voice and not hesitate to obey. The true life testimonies are awesome and inspiring."—Amazon reviewer

Jesus, your baby and you – A guide to trusting God during your pregnancy

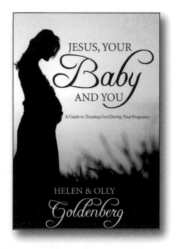

Why has God given you this child at this particular time? God's plans for your child were known before conception and God wants to meet with them whilst they are in the womb. The nurturing of their future calling begins in the womb.

Helen and Olly show us from the Bible that God is interested in the life of each person before they are born. With many real-life experiences and practical ideas they empower us to prepare ourselves, our babies and our whole family for a life together with God. Discover the tools you need to fight fear, build faith and trust God through your pregnancy and beyond.

> *"I'm so grateful for this book. It's helped my husband and I start our parenting from now. It's inclusive and accessible to readers in a number of different situations. It covers the areas often on the hearts and minds of expectant Mums and Dads. Reflective questions and practical tools are provided along the way, helping readers to put what they want into practice. I recommend!"—Amazon reviewer*

God's Generals for Kids series

The God's Generals for Kids series of biographies tell the miraculous and sometimes tragic story of men and women who have served God in recent history. These books are being used by God to stir up faith in the next generation of children.

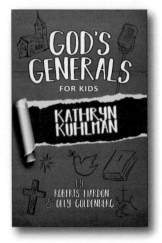

"These books changed my life." (Age 12)

"The children in our church have started to see miracles since reading these books."

"This is a wonderful series for parents and young children. We bought this series as a read along with our 7 year old. Not only is she able to read and comprehend the material it is written at a mature enough level have real substance."

"I've read this book over 7 times!" (Age 11)

God's Generals for Kids:

1. Kathryn Kuhlman
2. Smith Wigglesworth
3. John Alexander Dowie
4. Maria Woodworth-Etter
5. Evan Roberts
6. Charles Parham
7. William Seymour
8. John G. Lake
9. Aimee Semple McPherson
10. William Branham
11. A. A. Allen
12. Jack Coe

Contact:

Olly Goldenberg

BM Children Can

London

WC1N 3XX.

www.childrencan.co.uk

www.ahwg.co.uk

info@childrencan.co.uk